STROKE
NO JOKE

STROKE
NO JOKE

What are you going to do with what's left?

poetic images photography

Luther Moore

iUniverse®

STROKE NO JOKE
What are you going to do with what's left?

Scripture marked AKJV is from the Authorized King James Version of the Bible (the KJV), the rights in which are vested in the Crown in the United Kingdom and is reproduced here by permission of the Crown's patentee, Cambridge University Press.

The Cambridge KJV text, including paragraphing, is reproduced here by permission of Cambridge University Press.

iUniverse books may be ordered through booksellers or by contacting:

iUniverse
1663 Liberty Drive
Bloomington, IN 47403
www.iuniverse.com
1-800-Authors (1-800-288-4677)

ISBN: 978-1-4917-7346-8 (sc)
ISBN: 978-1-4917-7347-5 (e)

Library of Congress Control Number: 2015912936

Print information available on the last page.

iUniverse rev. date: 09/03/2015

To all the people who are faced with serious illnesses. I urge them to not give up, to maintain their faith, and to gain strength, and I remind them that they can and will make it if it is not their time to exit. I am living proof that we can overcome serious illnesses by having faith in ourselves and the willpower not to give up. I used that inner strength God gave me, which enables me to make vital changes in my life and be an inspiration to others.

To my loving parents, David and Earlease Moore; my children, Keith, Kenny, Kelley, Kevin, and Keenan Moore; my children's mom; and my brothers and sisters, Jack, Bernard, Sallie, Evelyn, Beverly, Priscilla, and Opal. I also dedicate this book to my deceased sister, Johnnie Mae, and my deceased brothers, Robert, Billy, and (my twin) Lewis.

—Luther Moore

CONTENTS

PREFACE

Hi, my name is Luther Moore, and I am the author of the book *Stroke No Joke*. I was born in a small town in South Carolina. I resided in New Jersey for many years. There, I was married and fathered five children from that marriage. I love to write songs, and I had a great time writing the book you see before you.

Stroke No Joke depicts my struggles related to a massive stroke that I had in May 1995. The doctors counted me out and said I would not have a good quality of life once I started to recover. I took stock of what the doctors had said, but I took greater stock in the promises and the power of God. My relationship with God is why I am here today. My spirit has led me to memorialize my struggle to have as normal of a life as I possibly could, and I know I was called by God to tell my story so that I could encourage and influence others.

For more information, please feel free to contact me at strokenojoke@bellsouth.net.

During the writing of this book and its passage from the spoken word to the written form, my good friend and mentor has been my Creator, to whom I am deeply grateful and whom I earnestly thank. I also express my indebtedness to my friends, Mr. Anthony Lewis, and family; my advisor and marketing wizard; my editor; and the many people who have freely supported my efforts.

CHAPTER 1

THE START OF THE FALL

August 8, 1988

After a fairly good day at work, I arrived home, relaxed a while, got a bite to eat, and then changed into my gym clothes to go for a much-needed workout. While sitting on the side of my bed, I suddenly experienced my entire body retaining fluid. I could not believe what was happening to me. It did not seem real. I felt no pain, dizziness, or anything abnormal. The swelling was moving at a rapid pace. I could not understand what was going on, so I waited a while to see if the swelling would stop, but within an hour or so, my weight had ballooned from 213 to 259 pounds. I felt like I was going to float away any second.

There was no plausible explanation in my mind at that time for why this was happening. I felt great, but my body was retaining fluid and swelling so fast I felt as though I were going to burst. I drove myself to the Barnet Hospital emergency room. The doctor could not tell me what was causing me to retain fluid until they ran some tests. They asked me several questions about any unusual foods I had eaten and drug use. There was nothing I had eaten or drunk that was not normal for me, and there were definitely no drugs in my system. They admitted me to the hospital, and I was kept there for some tests, including a kidney biopsy on Monday morning. To the best of my knowledge, Dr. Gupta performed the tests, and within a couple of days, he returned with my test results.

I was diagnosed with lupus. While in the hospital, I did a brief study on lupus and found that it is an autoimmune disorder and affects the organs and systems such as the skin, joints, and internal organs. Lupus can affect both men and women. The typical age range for someone to get lupus is ten to fifty years of age. It is more common in people of African and Asian descent. Lupus is usually hereditary, but in some cases, like mine, there is no familial history of the disease. To my knowledge, no one in my family had suffered from lupus. This disease turns the body's defenses against the body itself. Lupus occurs when antibodies attack the healthy cells in the body. Studies have found that certain drugs can cause lupus as well. It has been heavily researched and has been linked to other disorders but only in theory; nothing is definitely stated as fact. Symptoms of this can vary and occur in a wide array of areas in the body.

In the musculoskeletal system, it affects the joints and causes mild to severe joint pain, such as arthritis in the hands. The skin is affected by rashes, lesions, and painful nodules that appear to be raised bruises. The kidneys produce protein deposits, and renal failure, leading to dialysis, is a possibility. The nervous system can be damaged, causing headaches, mental dysfunction, seizures, and psychosis. Blood clots can occur and cause a pulmonary embolism.

Chest pain and shortness of breath are also symptoms. Endocarditis, which is the inflammation of the serous membrane that lines the cavities of the heart, and myocarditis, which is the inflammation of the muscular substance of the heart, can also arise. Pleurisy, affecting the delicate serous membrane in the thorax, can also occur as a result of lupus.

I remained in the hospital for a little over a month. Throughout that period, I felt great. *It was amazing how good*

I felt. I had no pain, only discomfort from the weight gain. I used that time to try to figure out how to prepare myself for when I returned home. I wanted to continue living on my own. I had to make some life-changing decisions if I wanted independent living to continue.

I had never really heard of this disease until I was diagnosed. Most sources of information on lupus seemed to be addressed to women. I guessed this was an equal-opportunity disease. I had to make some drastic changes in my lifestyle. Regarding my diet, I made sure to eat right. I had to continue my physical therapy. Staying busy really helped me. Staying out of the sun as much as possible was mandatory.

Eventually, I was released from the hospital to take on this new challenge in my life.

When I returned home, I rested for a few weeks. I was very weak, and my weight had dropped tremendously. I had no balance, and my memory had been affected. It was very difficult for me to walk, but I started working out again shortly after my release. I made sure that I ate right and got my proper rest to regain my weight and my strength so I could focus on getting my life back on track. I was determined not to let my condition break my spirit and definitely not to let it defeat me. Approximately six months or so after being released from the hospital, I returned to work on very light duty.

I was still weak and very thin, but I was determined to get my life back on track. I had to focus on empowering myself and accepting this new lifestyle, which included changing to a low-sodium diet. That meant reading labels for sodium content. It was a must in order for me to get well. I was not to expose myself directly to the sun, especially in the hottest part of the day. If I did, I would feel as if pins were sticking me all over my body. Physical weakness was something new for me. I was used to getting up every day, getting dressed, walking out of the door, and loving the sun. Humans are creatures of habit, and my habit was being outside for leisure and for work. I was the assistant maintenance supervisor for public housing, so I went in and out of the various buildings throughout the day, interacting with contractors and workers all day on the grounds. Being so cautious and staying out of the sun seemed to be an impossible task. I was in unfamiliar territory for life, but I had been given a second chance, and I was not going to abuse God's grace.

The most difficult obstacle to overcome was having the realization that God had given me the courage and it was up to me to make the best of it. I had to set aside my pride. Life is nothing but adjustments all of our lives, but some of them can be drastic and some of them can be terrifying. I had to make those changes, trust in a loving creator, and believe I could still learn to live a somewhat normal life, even facing a difficult disease.

Every disease is difficult. Every disease is scary. Sometimes, diseases affect some of us in different ways. People will turn and walk away, not knowing how to act or how to react to you. Once I was awakened to this, my attention quickly focused, and I stayed in control, maintaining a good attitude, keeping my doctors' appointments, and following instructions. All the while, I continued reading as much information on this disease as I could, hoping that would help me deal with the condition as I continued living life as normally as possible, making adjustments when necessary. I was amazed at the different advice given to me from various doctors. All of the advice was given with the statement that it was mandatory for my recovery.

Most of the doctors who treated me helped me to realize that I too was learning from my own reading and studies.

I understood quickly that the doctors did not have the answers that I needed so very badly. I do not believe that "studies" really had a clue as to how to deal with this disease at the time I was diagnosed. Much of the information that was given to me was not even close to helping with the symptoms that I was experiencing.

There was only one diagnosis but so many different suggestions on how it would affect my life and how I was to handle it. The most accurate advice that was given to me during those early stages was to stay indoors and cover up when outside in the hottest part of the day, because the sun is one of a lupus patient's worst enemies. I had to cut back on my sodium intake, which was not an easy task. However, it was imperative that I do so and keep myself encouraged after discovering all the life changes I had to make. I really had to stay strong for the things to come.

God had already prepared me for this transition in my mind. The paranoia tried to creep into my life, but I was not having that. No matter what it took, I was not allowing myself to stop living. I would not allow myself to give in. After a while, the information that I had read on the subject educated me instead of terrified me. I believe my life was spared to handle this and I will not be defeated. Maybe one day research will find a cure. That is my most fervent hope. This has been an eye-opener, getting my physical and mental attention quickly! I want to be capable of taking care of myself, and helping others is foremost within my mind, which makes all things seem easier.

This is my life, and I choose to live it, not to hear the word *lupus* and sit within a circle of self-loathing and pity. Rising above the disease, I keep my head held high, relying upon a merciful God who loves me and taking refuge in the sanctuary He gives with his loving heart. I know He would never have allowed me to have this disease if I was not able to use it to be a vessel, showing His goodness and mercy and teaching others who have diseases that are misdiagnosed. I had to fully understand how to stand tall and firm, remaining in control of my mind and in control of my choices. I chose to make a difference in someone else's life and help others who were striving to make themselves better. Seeing my reflection within a mirror, I felt God's love within my heart. I knew that He was always with me, encouraging me through every day and lending me strength to continue on. Whenever I see someone who is downtrodden, I ask if I may have a moment. When we discuss our lives, we learn strengths, not only in others, but our own strengths. I use every day to be a vessel for God, a vessel of encouragement, a living example of how to be the change you wish to see in the world.

My favorite saying is "Attitude determines your altitude," and it does, whether you realize this or not. This is a beneficial knowledge for existence that I pray more people are willing to understand. That is the catch-22, if you will. You must be willing to understand and recognize this within yourself. If you do not acknowledge this, you cannot grow and understand the divine purpose that God is wishing for your life. It did not take much thinking for me to figure this one out. We are much smarter and stronger than we think we are. When your life is on the line, your mental strength will take over. I started concentrating on where I was and what it would take for me to handle this challenge in my life.

A disease is a challenge of mental toughness. I must maintain a winning spirit, setting aside the fear by handing it over to God; this is my life. I have what I have, and I will win. I am going to stay strong against any thoughts that suggest this disease is a death sentence. Any disease can be a death sentence. It depends upon how you choose to react to being told you have a disease. I believe what happened to me is a message for others to learn from. I will not be disabled. I firmly disagree with that thought and others like it because that makes God look small instead of the great *giant* that He is. I would be my own worst enemy if I were to focus on my condition. I firmly believe that I can and I definitely will overcome this disease. If not, I will still make it.

This disease is a test of my spirit. You must have an understanding that there is never any provision without a problem having been there first. If I were to hold back, waiting until it looked like life was a problem-free journey, I would never know my potential, nor would I live a productive life. When I first heard about lupus, I took it lightly, thinking to myself that it was a horrific disease for any person to suffer through. Then I was diagnosed. In the beginning of my lupus diagnosis, I was already exercising every day, which was a plus for me. I had always loved challenges, but this was life changing and potentially life threatening.

I knew if God kept me, I could handle it. It is all about my attitude. I had a lot of work and studying pertinent information on the disease of lupus to do. I would not allow it to overwhelm me with what I heard from others or what I had read concerning the disease.

My focus is and will always be on caring for myself through a potentially devastating disease.

I just want to understand the seriousness of the disease and what should be avoided or what people with lupus should be aware of other than sunlight and sodium. This is the way life is. It can change in the blink of an eye. We are always just one heartbeat away from death. I was given a second chance at life if I wanted it. I know my life will never be as I once knew it. I will have challenges I will have to overcome, but I will not be labeled disabled.

There is an alternative. I will play the hand that I was dealt gratefully, and I will win. I will do whatever I have to do to stay alive and continue independent living with this obstacle; it has become a stepping stone and further strengthens my faith in God. I have gotten where I am today and feel as good as I do because of the right attitude and hard work. That is simply the way life is. At times, doors that seem to be closed permanently can reopen widely enough to get through with the fruits of faith. Through labor, I can reclaim my health, peace of mind, serenity, and tranquility.

I always remember that faith is only my mind or, in other words, "Now is the substance of things hoped for, the evidence of things not seen" (Hebrews 11:1 AKJV). I have to always keep an open mind concerning my condition, overcoming all obstacles or circumstances that get in my way. I am not an overly religious person, but I believe in God and I find strength in what I do. Believe me, the word is not so difficult to understand. It's life just waiting to be activated, if one so chooses. I believe this situation is a test for me. At the start of the fall, I believed I could and would overcome this condition and make it through this journey, which seemed impossible until I came to understand that my attitude and my work ethic would be what got me through this challenge. With what I have left inside of me, I can make it. If I put my mind to it, I can live a normal life. I have already seen myself on the other side of this situation. I will get there if I just stay focused.

I believe this part of my life was designed for this experience, and as I venture on through this journey, I will understand more fully life's worth. I have so much more living to do. I embrace my situation, and with God's grace,

I will make it and resume my independence. This has been a very difficult time in my life, but I know it will turn out to be the most rewarding. I am living a more purposeful life since the diagnosis and definitely a more focused one.

I hope that I have left a positive image in the mind of everyone I have come in contact with since this journey began. It truly has given me something to share and challenges that I will never forget if I live to be a thousand years old. If life doesn't give up on me, I will not lose my zeal for living. I will continue in a positive direction with what life gives me. Sometimes things happen in our lives that we have no control over, but our determination can get us through. I have truly found out who I really am as a man. There were times when I did not want to know because I knew it was going to be a fight trying to activate that winning spirit that I knew existed inside of me.

I can always feel it as long as I stay focused. When I give that extra effort, it always opens doors that no one can close but me. If God made it available, how do I know this to be so? Because there have been things that have happened over and over during my recovery that I could not have gotten through otherwise; nothing else could have given me the strength or allowed that but God's grace. I believe He saw me doing things that were required in order to recover and He stepped in and kept blessing me every day in some way, allowing me to continue on this journey. To me, that seemed supernatural because I didn't give up. I maintained the integrity, character, and work ethic that were required, and in return, He continually promoted me. Even when things seem to be working against me, I keep making progress.

There was never a doubt in my mind that I would make it. I felt like a giant was on my back every step of the way, but God's love kept me on track. Living with lupus is no joke, and staying positive, staying focused, keeping a strong mind, and being courageous are necessary. Never say, "I can't." Confront whatever you have to with these weapons: trust in God, a positive attitude, a good relationship with your doctor, and trust in yourself—and you will succeed. I want other patients to know that having lupus is not a death sentence. You *can* live a normal life.

The most important thing of all is your attitude. You have to want to live. Despite the difficulties I am facing, I still have hope, and you should also. There are wonderful people making tremendous contributions to finding a cure. When I was first diagnosed, I kept a positive attitude, even after finding out how seriousness the disease is, I did not let myself lose sight of what I wanted to accomplish. Every day, I thank God for giving me this opportunity. I am thankful to be a vessel being used to continue spreading the message of His love and goodness, and I tell others that He is willing to provide for all of us.

I am still here on this beautiful earth because He chose me for a few more days, and I am grateful. This situation has never been about me. I take it one day at a time, maintaining a positive attitude. If I had chosen to be negative, thinking only negative thoughts and having only negative feelings, my body would have reacted thusly and I would not be where I am today. I realized that I control my own destiny to some extent. I have not allowed myself to sit around complaining and feeling sorry for myself. If I have to carry this for the rest of my life, that is okay. As I recover, I would enjoy participating in some form of research and helping others to overcome or learn to accept where they are.

Death is inevitable, sick or well, so why waste positive energies on something that is inevitable regardless? I don't take my condition or my life lightly, but I maintain a positive outlook on reality. I only get one shot at life, so I get up each day with grand expectations and motivation and shoot for the moon. If I miss, I may land among the stars. While I am alive, I want to be productive first for myself and then for my children and people in general.

We live, and then we die, whether we have a medical condition or not, so why complain? I hope when I leave this earth, I am totally exhausted from living my life on my terms to the fullest. I will not use up positive energies complaining and worrying about something I can't change. I am happy. I feel good, if not great. Lupus could have really terrified me because of my organs being involved, but while I am alive, I am going to be a terror on life in a positive way. Don't get me wrong; I do the things I need to do. I stay away from things that are not good for me or may worsen my condition. For now, I am handling my situation very well, and that helps me live life passionately one day at a time. Maybe one day, we'll all be able to feel like lupus is a fading memory.

Lupus is not the terribly debilitating disease it once was. Many newly diagnosed people are frightened by the fact that it is a terminal disease. All that matters to me is that I am still alive after being diagnosed twenty years ago. I really don't have any limitations that burden me, nothing that hinders me. I don't know what is next for me. As long as life continues to grace me with its presence, I will give my all every day. I really feel good, and I try to inspire people each day in my travels. That's my concern as I proceed on my journey.

Since my diagnosis with lupus, I have become stronger physically and mentally. This illness is complex, confusing, and complicated at times. However, I continue to stay positive in my workouts and take seriously concerns about staying out of the hot sun and eating right as much as possible. I will be all right. I know that it is God in action in all phases of my recovery, and I have to use good sense concerning my condition. I have been blessed in every way imaginable concerning my health. I cannot get out of this world alive, so I will accept what I have as a blessing, thank God, and continue to move forward. I can still make my life adventurous. If I stay focused, maybe I can help others realize their potential and learn to enjoy life as it hurls toward them so they don't choose to drown themselves in self-pity. Mine is the other side of that coin.

The disease seemingly chose me, but I can handle my part in this, as long as God continues to bless me with His graces. I don't let my situation intimidate me or dictate how I will live the rest of my life. I am good in spirits, confident, and doing whatever I have to do. I hope I am inspiring others as I journey forward. I will live, not just survive, as long as I stay alive. This is only a test, and as long as I maintain a winning spirit and am willing to dig deeper inside of myself daily with a thankful attitude, I believe that I can win and bless others. I give 110 percent of myself to my situation every day. I thank God for giving me such strong parents. The time I had with them was short but so special. I know I have done so well because of the strength I saw demonstrated through my parents. I truly believe they have been watching over me from the start. As I journey on my way, they stay connected to my spirit and help me to keep my spirit strong. Just thinking of them keeps me focused. I can see the both of them any time I choose through my mind's eye. I can see them easily. I realize how crazy that sounds, but it's true. I am hoping that I have left a trail for my children like my parents left for me. I hope they will be able to overcome whatever adversities they may encounter and they can be a beacon of light for their kids and others to follow.

Life is tough, but it is such a joyous experience even when difficult times arise. If we don't quit, we can make it. You can make it. Just remember this: we are God's creation. Do not ever put limits on what God can do through you. When you give up, you are limiting yourself and God. We are winners. Your attitude will be the determining factor in whether your condition makes or breaks you. I am a winner. There is no quit in me. Being diagnosed with lupus has only enhanced my strength and my willingness to stay strong and maintain confidence in whatever I do. I don't know what is ahead for me, but as I journey on through life, I hope that I will maintain my independence. Whatever I face in the future, as long as God keeps blessing me, I will find the strength to keep myself motivated, just as I have in the past. This has been hard but so amazing.

I thank God for the opportunity and for keeping me strong and confident in dealing with this illness. I know that it will always be a part of my life, but I will win! I thank God for making this such an amazing journey.

I Can Do This

"I can do this." Those were the first slurred words with any meaning out of my mouth after I realized that I had had a stroke. I had been in a coma for seven or eight days. I don't know how long it took me to regain full consciousness, but when I did, I knew I would make it through this trauma. My body was weak, but my mind was strong. I believed that this was only a test that I had been chosen for. Everything that I would need to recover I had. I knew if I stayed focused, I would not fail. *I can do this.* The more I processed that thought in my mind, the more it energized my spirit. My mind and what brain power I had left strengthened me.

Sometimes I could hear my spirit in a soft voice saying, "You can do this. You will be all right. You will be independent once again," and I believed that to be so.

Life is a challenge, a process. Things happen in life, but we can overcome them if we stay focused. That's just life. Challenging situations sometimes generate new energies and new opportunities. It's up to you to take advantage. You can do this. The load will seem heavy and unbearable at times, and you'll feel like giving up, but that will only drive you even more. I will continue to maintain the right attitude. I am a winner. I will win if I dare to stay faithful and motivated. I will succeed. I can do this. Faith has replaced all doubt and fear in my mind. If I stumble and fall, I will rise immediately to stand tall. In a moment, I will continue on my journey. I *can* do this.

I believe I was given the strength before the task. I will complete this journey. I am on the right path, and my life will be better because of this. I can do this. I can make the pieces fit like a hand in a glove. Life is designed that way. I don't worry about where the pieces fit; I just keep placing them where I think they do. I will know when they are in the right place. I just trust my instincts. If I listen to my mind, I will be okay. My mental clarity is improving daily, my concentration is getting better, and really focusing is getting easier. My memory is also getting sharper each day, and my learning ability is improving slowly. But surely I am learning how to process bits and pieces of information. I *can* do this!

One day, I came out of my apartment to retrieve something out of my vehicle—I can't remember exactly what it was—but when I reached into my pocket for my keys, I realized that I had my pants on backward. I immediately started laughing so hard at myself it brought tears to my eyes. It is things like that that give me confidence to keep going.

Small, silly incidents like that empower me every day to let me know that I am on the right track. I just can't give up. I know I am going to be all right. I understand what it will take for me to live with this situation. Even silly things I did gave me strength. They brought laugher to my spirit. I would be ready to walk out the door, and my shoes would be on the wrong feet. It was hard, but I would get a good laugh and I would keep on doing things wrong until I got it right. I wouldn't quit. This went on for a long time, but I kept busy, whether things turned out right or not. I was determined. I worked so hard that I started feeling sorry for myself, but little by little, I began getting things right sometimes. Eventually, things started getting a lot easier day by day. When my friend was around, I let her think I knew what I was doing, and she never knew. I kept saying, "I can do this. I know." She worried about me being left at home with my condition when she went to work. I know she worried all the time. That was why I moved out. I didn't want to stay and cause problems for her. I know I made the right decision. When things we do or don't do affect others we say we care about, sometimes we have to make the hard decisions. It is not always easy, especially when it is a good friend, because we experience so few true friends on this journey called life. This experience has been hard, but it's also the most amazing time of my life. I know I can do this and inspire others at the same time. Remember, my belief creates my thoughts, my thoughts generate feelings, and my feelings affect my body's healing system through my mind. I believe and trust in what I can do with my mind. I will come through. God really is in me and you, but we never realize just how close He really is to us until times like this. He still will not force Himself on you. He will come only through invitation, and I believe that nothing will be forced on me. It's my choice to let Him in.

A lot of my strength also comes from reflecting on the strength of my father. When He was alive, He was an amazing man. His right leg was amputated below the knee in 1958 or 1959 when I was ten or eleven years old, but I never heard him complain about anything. I was only fifteen years of age when he died from a stroke. I remember everything about him. His strength and his character were amazing. He is always vividly clear in my mind. Thinking of him quickens my spirit. After all these years, I guess that is where I get the strength to continue on this journey. He is always with me and was even before the stroke. I think of how short the time was that I spent with my mom and dad. I still feel their presence daily in my spirit. I remember something my dad used to always say to my twin brother: "Always try to find a job that you really like, and you will never have to work hard a day in your life, and as you mature, learn to work smart, not hard. You may have hard work to do sometimes, but learn how to work the job; don't let the job work you. Whatever you do, always give it your best. Whenever you have to redo a job, you have worked twice as hard and twice as long for the same results or the same pay. Always remember, whatever you do in life, it always says something about who you are as a person, as a man. It's the foundation that you lay and will follow you for life." That's why I will not give up. I will give this situation my best shot. The only thing that will guarantee the success of a potentially doubtful undertaking is faith from the beginning that I can do this. I will make it. I believe that when things happen in our lives, we are already prepared in advance to handle them. Now, that's a good thing, but some of us still never get it. We sit around and complain, waiting for God to fix it. He has already prepared us to handle whatever. That's the way life works. That's what I believe. I know he kept me for a reason. What I do with what I have left is up to me. I don't let negative and toxic people rent space in my head. This is a hell of an experience. I can do this. I won't let anybody steal what God has already guaranteed me in my spirit, if I want it. God is true to His word. We need to be true to what we say we believe. I truly believe I was chosen for this journey. And I will make it.

CHAPTER 2

STROKE NO JOKE

1995

It was the last week of April in 1995. I had a few annual days that I had to use by a certain time. I took off work that week. I made an appointment to see my doctor before returning to work May 4. I was given a clean bill of health. After arriving home about 6:20 p.m., I relaxed for a while, and then I got a bite to eat and sat in the den to watch TV. My friend was in the kitchen talking on the phone. I finished my food, washed my dish, and returned to the den to watch some more television. Suddenly, I lost the use of my right side. With me being the jokester that I am at times, my friend wasn't quick to take me seriously.

I tried to get her attention to let her know that something was wrong. But I could not speak. I could see her coming toward me after I had fallen onto the floor from the couch. I vaguely remember the paramedics arriving to transport me to the hospital. I remember someone standing over me as soon as I arrived at the hospital. They looked as though they were in a three-dimensional movie that I was watching without the glasses, and they seemed far away at the same time. I was semiconscious, and my memory was in and out. Suddenly, I lost all consciousness and went into a coma.

I was told later that I stayed in the coma for quite a while. After about a month or so, I started understanding a little of what was going on around me very slowly. Everything seemed different. I didn't know how to communicate. It seemed like a tremendous amount of time had passed, and I was in another time zone or place. Everything seemed new to me. I didn't know how to react to anybody or anything. I was badly confused. A while later, I was told I had been in a coma and I wasn't capable of understanding things for a while. It was hard trying to put words together or speak, but I kept pushing myself and still do, even to this day. My surroundings were unfamiliar. I felt as though I was in some strange place. I didn't know what to do. I couldn't think clearly. I felt closed in. This went on for a long time, but I felt good. I was still in the hospital, but I was recovering slowly.

On June 3, I was transferred to Kessler's Rehabilitation Center in Saddle Brook, New Jersey, to continue my therapy. I remained another month. The stroke really left me severely paralyzed throughout my entire right side, and I had aphasia, or loss of speech. My rehabilitation began with speech therapy and trying to help me understand what had happened to me and to help me regain some basic knowledge of life skills. My mouth felt as though it was in the wrong place. It was difficult trying to swallow. My occupational therapist worked tirelessly with me certain days, trying to help me understand what was going on because I was clueless.

My entire memory bank had to be reprogrammed to hold and understand information. It was difficult trying to learn how to walk up and down steps and how to transfer my right hand usage to my left side. It was hard because my senses were affected terribly. I was just like a baby trying to take his or her first step. I had speech therapy every day. I would slur my words badly. The therapy was more difficult than I had envisioned it would be. It was a challenge. I had a seemingly impossible task ahead of me, trying to recapture what I had lost and hold on to what I had left. Every day, I worked hard religiously. This will be ongoing, probably for the rest of my life. At that time, I was trying to regain some clarity and understanding of what was going on around me. For the time being, independence was gone and I wanted to go home.

It had been almost two months since I'd slept in my own bed. My therapy was transferred back to Barnet Hospital. After about three or four weeks, I asked my primary doctor to allow me to be released to do my own therapy, and he promised that he would be there for me if need be. I would not be where I am today in my recovery with the type of therapy they were administering to me. My intention is to recover completely, not just be alive. I want to live on my own terms. I didn't understand the doctor's concern or him not allowing me to attempt the exercises I wanted to do while in their care. I wanted some pain, but when I went out on my own, I understood the shape I was in physically. It was frightening.

My memory was not as good as I had thought, and I was not in the condition I thought I was in. It took a long time for me to regain my focus and enough energy to exercise and get positive results, but being on my own enabled me to try different things and understand why I was restricted while at Kessler's. When I reflect back to August 8, 1988, when I was first diagnosed with lupus, I realize I had no idea of the magnitude of this disease. It was much more devastating and much more serious than I had thought, but I would make it. Everything I needed to handle this illness was already inside of me, and things were getting clearer each day. It seemed as though I had already overcome the situation that was at hand. I would not stay in this shape depending on someone else to get me through; if I had to, I would not make it.

I would beat this and be able to help others in the process, and that would also strengthen me. I changed how I prepared my meals, limiting the sodium content. My food wasn't as good, but I had been a chef for a while in my earlier years, and as time progressed and my senses got better, I learned how to enhance the way my foods tasted without all that sodium. I experimented with other salt-free seasonings and ingredients, and my meals were starting to taste almost as good without sodium. (Yes, no sodium again.) It was mostly restricted from my diet. (I got it.)

Battling lupus is serious, but over time, I learned how to really manage my sodium intake. I was back to eating some of the foods that I already knew I should avoid, but I changed the preparation of them. In a lot of food, I find that the sodium content has been cut down in the marketplaces, which is good. Having lupus and having had a stroke because of it, heightened my concern about my sodium intake. Both conditions required me to watch my sodium intake. The lupus also made it difficult for me to be in the sun. At times, I would use sunscreen lotion, but I still had to be aware of how much direct sunlight I received in the hottest part of the day. As devastating as my condition was, there was something inside of me that just would not allow fear to enter my spirit. I knew from the way I felt that I would beat this or if not beat it, live my life with dignity.

With that on my mind, I learned this illness could be controlled to some extent; otherwise, I would have never made it back. Positive energy always produces positive results. That's why I will not give up. Sometimes, things happen in our lives that may take almost a lifetime to understand, and sometimes, we never understand them, but if we believe in ourselves and work hard, we can make it happen. I truly believe that things happen sometimes just to get our attention. What I am going through may help others who are faced with difficult challenges in their lives. I do know that I will never quit. It builds character. It strengthens and encourages me more every day. We can overcome much more than we think we are capable of. I did not understand that fact until my life was changed overnight. It was not a game. Three strikes, and you're out. A stroke is no joke, and it's definitely not a game. Now I live each day of my life like it is my last day. Even if you are taking care of yourself enough, events will still happen in life that you can't do anything about. My body and my mind are the control panel for my life. I will make it if I really want to. Sometimes, my memory doesn't serve me as well as it once did, but I won't quit working at full capacity to get my life back on track.

When I first returned home from the hospital, that's when reality really set in. Every day, I walked or did some type of exercise. My friend would walk with me sometimes, but whether she did or not, I would do what I had to do. We had been together approximately two and a half years. I had known her about fifteen years before the stroke. We had a great relationship even before we got together, but after I had the stroke, in my spirit, I never felt that she really wanted me there. That was why I moved. I could feel her attitude change, and that told me a lot, if I really wanted to know the truth. I didn't ever feel her support. I could handle my physical condition, but I could not handle being in a relationship and feeling alone at this time. When I would go walking and get back home so late at night, sometimes, I wondered if she really cared where I was or if I was okay or not.

I never let her know that was how I was feeling. I just kept doing what I had to do, trying to show her while I was there that I wasn't lazy and that I was trying to do whatever it took to get back on track. I would be standing in the yard not knowing what to do, but I refused to let her know what I was feeling and thinking. I really believe that she was glad when I left. I know I had an angel watching over me every second of the day. In writing this book, I can only give it to you the way I get it or the way it comes out. I am not going to fail and miss my blessing. It is tough, but that's life. The situation that I am faced with has given me so much strength. I say this so much because it's true. I believe that this was something I was chosen for, and I will not allow my self-esteem to erode with fear and destroy me. I don't know what the rest of the population would do, so I keep up the fight. I will make it. It's all about my attitude. I must stay in control. I want to live so I can encourage others. I am going through a life-changing situation, and I won't quit. I won't give up until my time is up.

My children have no idea the strength and the courage I have generated from them during my recovery. They played such an integral part in me maintaining my strength and my focus. They kept my motivation levels high. I don't think they have a clue how much energy I generated from them. I don't think that I would be alive today if they were not a part of my life. They weren't physically with me every day, but they knew my condition and that was enough to keep me motivated. I could not let them see me fail. I am their father, and I refused to let them see or hear me complaining about my condition. I don't see myself as a disabled person. I am temporarily inconvenienced. Sometimes, we give up before we even attempt to test the waters, and we rob ourselves based on circumstances without even trying. We become disabled out of pity for ourselves. All I need to recover I have it inside of me, waiting to be unleashed. This process has been the most inspirational time of my life.

Even though it has been hard work, it's a fair game. This is life. I have remained focused and positive. This test has become my best friend, my partner, my strength. I remember one day I was out doing my exercises, and it was terribly hot. I decided to walk up Temple Street Hill—and I do mean *hill*. I couldn't walk too well at that time, and my focus wasn't that good, but approximately twice a week, I walked about a mile and a half from where I lived to challenge a hill. It was really steep. That walk had become kind of a routine of mine.

This day was like no other day that I had walked this hill. It was hot, and about halfway up, I got so tired that I could hardly put one foot in front of the other. It was super hot but also humid. I still had quite a ways to go to reach the top. I stopped for a few minutes and looked up. It seemed as though the top of the hill was moving farther and farther away. I just wanted to get back home, but I knew what I had to do. Suddenly, I heard a vehicle approaching on my left. It stopped. It was my daughter. She got out of the car and approached me. I was about to pass out. She said, "Daddy, it's too hot for you to be out here in this sun. Let me take you home."

My reply was, "No, this is the only way I can put my life back together. I will be okay."

I was so tired I felt like I was going to pass out any minute, but she was not going to give me a ride. I was still her dad, and she was not going to convince me to get in that car that day. Finally, with tears in her eyes, she got into her car and drove off. I wanted to stop her so badly and get in that car. As the car started up the hill, I fell up against the nearest tree and said, "Lord, I wanted that ride so badly, but my kid, she cannot drive me. I am sorry, but that's the way I feel concerning all my children and I probably will always feel that way. I must stay strong for them even when I don't feel like it. They don't understand, but they will one day when they become parents. They will find strength they didn't think they had. It's a mother's and father's role in raising their kids. All the time, they have to be strong. Even when we don't feel like it, we have to stay focused and set examples." That day, when I was walking that hill, nothing was more important to me than making that point. It was so important to me especially at that time in my life. My children would continue to be my motivation.

My kids have been the driving force behind my recovery, and as they have gotten older and started their own families, they have found and will find strength within themselves in certain circumstances. They will come through when it comes to their kids. That day on that hill, when my daughter approached me, she definitely will come to understand. Obstacles that seem impossible to us come into our lives, and I guarantee you they will come through. Life will strengthen you or kill you. That's just the way it is, because that's life. All of us are so uniquely made, and we are so much stronger than we think. On this journey, I hope that every day I have given my children something to think about through my recovery. As they travel on their journeys through life, that courage will become their best friend and strengthen them as it did me. It will keep them strong. Life is no joke; believe me.

Independences is life, and I refused to give mine up without a fight. As long as there is breath in my body, I know I can make it. Sometimes, we lose the battle when we stop fighting. There is a winner in all of us. When things get tough, we have to get tougher. That's just the way life is designed. I get stronger every day, and that's just living by faith. I keep my mind on God, and He guides me and tells me in my spirit that I am capable of climbing this mountain so long as I don't give up. If I stay positive, I will reach the top. I was not supposed to make it. Some doctors weren't optimistic at all about my recovery, but they are not God. Being a doctor is only their profession. I received my confirmation from the giver of life that I was going to make it. Don't get me wrong; my doctors were amazing, but they have limitations when it comes to life. You have to know what to block out for yourself when your life is at stake.

Life experiences can be a teacher, but you must be willing to do the hard things and know that what you have left inside is more than enough to start over if you want to. I had one choice. That was to get busy. I am so proud of how I have handled my condition. This has been a phenomenal ride. *My attitude has been so positive.* I'm not saying this journey has been easy, because it hasn't, but it has been an experience that I will never forget as long as I live. It has been so inspirational. I have maintained a winning attitude every day and remind myself how blessed I am just to be alive. I will return to independent living. It takes hard work, but with purposeful directions, I will succeed.

The more positive I remain, the more I realize the impact it will have on my recovery. At times, we can be placed in a devastating but blessed situation, and we complain it away because it seems to be to intimidating or different. We give up. Instead, we have to reach deep down inside of ourselves in order to reach up and get what's in reserve inside of us. My life is being threatened. I believe there is something inside all of us that's reserved just for such an occasion. If I want to win, I must not be too patient when it comes to saving my life. I must be willing. It's only then that I can activate the winning spirit that's within me. Being angry only robs me of what I have left. It takes willingness to gain courage and courage to gain strength, but it's left up to me. God left me here, and I believe it is for a reason and purpose. I refuse to give up. So I work on making sure I maintain a winning attitude and gain courage to reach the altitude that's needed to overcome what I am facing. There are so many things in life we may never understand why they happen, but I am still alive. I still have a chance to challenge life, and there's still no guarantee I will make it, only a possibility that I will remain my life's friend just a little longer—if it's God's will.

I believe there is a *divine* purpose in what happened to me. Maybe one day I will understand this even better. I really believe this had to happen to me for the next chapter of my life. This has been hard work. Believe me, life has a way of getting your attention quickly. I believe that all of God's creation will be tested one day in some way or another, and it's up to us whether we pass the test or not. It is on us, so as Marvin Gaye says, "Let's get it on!" That's just the way life is.

I tried to stay on track with my thinking, and things started getting clearer for me after I stopped trying to second-guess God. I had a stroke, and I am still standing strong with the strength that I have left within me. I didn't know half of what I was capable of overcoming until that moment of truth. We are so uniquely made; we are so much stronger than we think we are. Sometimes, we don't make it because we are just lazy. Life is expressed through us, but at times, we just don't get it. We think life is indebted to us, but we are indebted to life; we owe everything to life. We are not here just for the ride, and as I traveled, exploring life's experiences, I was told within my spirit that I could make it back if I wanted to. It was up to me. I could do it. It takes determination and belief in myself. *I listened to my spirit.* I have so much left inside to contribute to life and to the world that I haven't even touched on yet. If I just listen and don't give up, I can win. It's not my time to exit, but it's up to me to make that distinction. I have learned so much from my condition. The brain is a very flexible and capable human instrument. I decided to make an honest effort during my recovery to resume making beautiful music with life and showing others that if you get knocked down in life and don't get knocked out, you can get up and resume living life. You just have to *maintain the right attitude and apply that winning spirit you will need to regain your strength.* I took control and am moving on.

The most important thing for me, as I keep saying, is staying focused and believing that I can come back if I don't give up. We really need to understand when our life changes and our body's protective system goes to work that it teams up with the mind and the communication system centered in the brain governed by the mind and our spirit. I read a story a while ago about a woman who made it to her physician and said that if he found something terribly wrong with her, she didn't think she could handle it. I thought the same thing when I first had the stroke and was in a coma. I was told after recovery the doctors did not think that I would live, but they were wrong. I did not understand anything for a long time, but when I did, I didn't want to die. I had to start life over. When I returned home from rehabilitation, I had to retrain my brain; I could have given up, but for me, it was a hell of a challenge. My liability became my greatest asset because it was in my spirit to win. I wanted to live and be independent. I told her, "You can too." I made the effort that was needed to overcome. I will find a way. There is something special inside all of us, which we discover when we are put to the test. We always have more in reserve than we think we do. I can do this, but it won't be easy. The power of the mind is our attitude to shape, influence, and alter reality. It is enormous, provided we believe it's possible within us. Too often, we give in, but affirmation works because it actively engaged my will, helping me to overcome and eventually silence that inner voice that kept telling me the contrary, that I could not come through this and I didn't want it! The approach is astonishingly simple, yet it's based on a profound truth.

The power of the mind and my attitude is key. Try it. They must work together. I read somewhere that life is 10 percent what happens to you and 90 percent how you react to it, and so it is with me. I am in charge of my attitude. I made up my mind that I could handle my situation. It's my life at stake. Somehow, things that were so hard to do started becoming a little easier day by day. I only get one shot at life. A stroke is no joke, but it has really *inspired me*.

This life is the only one that I get. My health and my healing can be made better or worse by what I do with what I have left. Every day, I remind myself that I have a healthy mind. It strengthens my defenses against any further toxins that I might encounter. I feel this is in my control. I tell myself what I want to accomplish pertaining to my health, and I stay in control. It's all in my mind, and I trust it. When I believe and stay focused, I will get stronger every day, no matter what the circumstances might be. There is a kind of inner calmness and peace. An undefeatable attitude cannot fail to exercise a mighty power over the human body.

Because the good things in life teach us that the creator and giver of life must be good, it is possible for anyone to believe some of these good things, but the person who knows the love of God can live a life illuminated by the light of faith. It is this full view of goodness and grace and positive outcome that's called the truth. The truth, He says, will set us *free*. That's why I believe I am doing so well. I knew that

I would make it. I could feel it. I was kept for a reason. Do you think that God is good and in control? What do you tell yourself when life gets tough, plans fail, finances get tight, or sickness strikes? I never worried whether I would make it through this situation or not.

I felt that I would all through my body. I felt like what had happened to me was predestined, like it was a continuation of what had happened to me in August 1988. It did not feel like the years in between the two had passed. They seemed so closely connected. I mean, in time, I didn't feel threatened or that my life would be taken at any time. Believe me, there was something in my spirit that assured me I was going to be all right. I believe hope is a choice, and I choose hope, not hopelessness. That's why I believe I am doing as well as I am. This is no time to back up; this is no time to be discouraged. This is the time to process what happened to me. This is a time to ask God for strength and to show me the way forward and who I really am in Him so I know what I am capable of.

This is the time to find out what I am made of; I have seen myself through this, and seeing is believing. With hard work, I can overcome this. I am running over with enthusiasm because I was given another chance. I am going to be strong. My thoughts are positive every day. My mind is getting stronger, and I really care what happens to me. I firmly reject the thought that I am disabled and others like it. I have had so much pain and joy dealing with this situation. I am an older man, but I don't want to look back on my life and see an old man who didn't try. I want to be able to say, "I made it. I got here because I believed and worked hard whether I was consciously thinking of it or not. I believed only in that which can heal and inspires me through seemingly insurmountable problems."

I would like to become a launching platform for others to have faith in themselves. I wanted my faith to guarantee me the energy that I needed to promote this human vehicle so that it will grant me a little more life. I won't give up. I am just on the other side of a great calm. I am living proof and reminded every day that I am equipped to complete this journey. I am a winner. I feel that I was chosen for this so that I am able to help others. I know that everything that I will need is available and waiting for me every day, as I need it, and I try to exhaust it. His wisdom releases power in my life every day. If I don't use my muscles and my mind, they will inevitably atrophy.

I have mental and spiritual muscles, which must be exercised also; if my thoughts, attitude, motivation, and reactions are not godlike, my contract with God, I believe, is broken and I will become disabled, depressed, more dejected, and fearful. I have to look within every day. What I need to make it through is already in me. I wanted to live so I can inspire others, and that is my mission every day. Through *Stroke No Joke*, I want to give you three words that have been helping me transform my life and get back on track: "Do not complain." I believe that God kept me here to inspire others. While on this journey, I can see the works of faith in my mind. This opportunity is a chance to overcome. It is an almost unbelievable journey that seems too difficult to fathom. It took me a while to realize the miracle that was surrounding me. It had to be. I could not have made it any other way. You have to know. Sometimes I get a feeling like no other that I have ever felt in my life. You too can take what you have left and use it. You have to know that you have the courage and the strength within yourself and learn how not to just sit and wait for God to give you things He has already equipped you with. Sometimes, when things happen in our life and we think we can't make it, maybe just maybe, it's a test designed specifically for us.

Life is a challenge, an opportunity for you to discover your hidden talents. I know you have heard that many times before in certain situations, but it applies to all of us. When I emerged from the coma, it took almost two years for me to really start understanding that God had kept me for a reason that I know not of at this moment. I will not blow it by complaining. What I do with it is my gift to God. I have learned that whatever season we are in, God wants us to know and say, "I can do this but not on my own strength." I say this from my heart and from my own devastating experiences. When you find yourself experiencing things that seem impossible to overcome, maybe it's your miracle. Trust it. Nothing is beyond your ability unless you try to overcome it on your very own. When you trust God, He is always at work, demonstrating His great power for you through you.

Miracles only happen when we partner with God, so take what you have left and stop complaining. Again, you might surprise yourself. Sometimes our weaknesses can be our strength. We can be strong in certain areas and struggling in others, yet God can still use us regardless. I have had a heck of a ride putting my life back together. I didn't know what I had inside of me just waiting to be unleashed on life. It's so amazing how things unfolded at the right time and allowed me to realize my strengths. I am blessed to be where I am today. I still have a ways to go, but I will make it. Right at this very moment, I am speaking to so many others who are allowing themselves to become victims just sitting around waiting on God for their healing or miracle to put their life back together. You already have it. All you need to do is get up out of that bed or that chair you are just lying or sitting in every day doing nothing for yourself. There is a price we must pay, which is hard work, but you can do it. The reason so many people are stuck where they are and never make it back when things happen to them is that they have so many excuses, questions, or doubts instead of stepping out on faith and believing in themselves. There is no risk for me. This has been the most inspirational time of my life. The ability to hear God and the ability to believe what I have heard and apply it to my life is awesome.

With everything in me, I will apply myself and complete this mission. I believe that all things are possible for you and for me with our all-powerful God. Life has been so hard for the last few years for me, but it has been the most inspirational time of my life. I am not trying to impress you; I'm just telling it like it is. I have been so blessed, and I have gained much more than I lost. I found out so many things about myself and how God's word works through me or us if we allow it to. The thrill of fulfillment is so sweet and rewarding, and the satisfaction I feel is always increased by the fact that I knew I could do this and was willing to work for it no matter how hard it is. I have to press on, always following that quiet voice in my spirit. In any case, it's never too loud. God's time is perfect. He is never late, not even by one millisecond. Believe that. So when things get hard in your life—I hope not from foolishness on your part—try to stay focused and He'll bring you through. Believe me; we are that human vehicle that God works through. I used to see people with disabilities and wonder what I would do if I were in their shoes. Could I overcome or handle a situation like they were in? I constantly thought about things like that when I was a young. I said I could beat that, not knowing what my future held for me. Now I have a chance to prove to myself what I always wondered about; life is full of surprises.

Sometimes I wonder if I had the stroke to test my faith, my will to see what I would do; God is true to His word, and God's word is true.

When I had the stroke, after I got to where I could understand, there was something put inside of me almost immediately. It was like a guarantee was placed in my spirit that I was going to be all right and I would not fail if I didn't quit. I would live on my own terms if I didn't mind the work. I was too stubborn to just lie down and die or be in a wheelchair. That was not in my makeup. In my mind, I was already healed. I wanted to live. I wanted to fulfill the vision God had placed in my spirit. I knew I could make it through this situation, but complaining was not going to do it. I had to stay focused, and I could conquer this challenge.

I really felt that God had His hand on me. I never needed to second-guess that. Regardless of my circumstances, I always kept this in mind. I am trying to save my life. It's always too soon to quit. My decision was to make this opportunity a success so others could see God's awesomeness through me. I don't have to be a victim of my circumstances. Sometimes, it is a matter of personal choice whether we can overcome what we are faced with or not.

CHAPTER 3

DISORIENTED?

1996

In April 1996, approximately one year since having the stroke, I was alert but still confused for a while. I felt that an independent life was totally over for me. I was so disoriented and not able to think clearly or know one day from the other at times, but I refused to accept that as a defeat. Every day, I kept pushing with everything in me. I still could not speak clearly, and most of all, I felt alone. There was no one on the face of God's green earth who really understood what was going on in my mind, not even me.

This was a time of massive confusion for me because I didn't know what my future held or if I would even have one again after the damage to my brain. I was easily distracted and confused about where I was or how to proceed. I was also uncertain as to directions. My confusion was characterized by lack of clarity, and the lupus had affected my organs. I did feel at times that I would not be able to overcome certain challenges. But every day, I kept moving forward. I would not stop. Sometimes, I would think about how long I might live with this condition, if I didn't give up, but the only thing I could do at this moment was to work with what I had left and try to build on it by giving my body constant vigorous exercises, even though my coordination was really bad as I tried to remember the exercises I was doing daily.

I couldn't keep them on my brain, so whatever would come to me, I would do. I kept busy. Before the stroke, I could hold cars or keep them from moving. My strength was amazing. Now I was trying to reclaim my strength and my identity. I was hoping to regain my independence once again, which was all gone for the moment. I was now someone who had to depend on others to some extent for my survival. Regardless of how temporary it might be, this was the most frustrating time for me. I cannot begin to understand how people can just give up on life. I know that I had a stroke, but giving up was so far from my mind. I once read that your brain works like an instrument; like a piano, it connects to your spirit and mind.

It influences the body's actions and profoundly influences the mind. The mind is great enough to help make you sick or help you get well. Changes in your spirit can affect your mind and your body. I was disoriented, but for some reason, one thing stayed clear in my mind. *I can do this,* I thought. Based on things that I can do, God gives me the will to keep pushing. Most of us go through life without ever knowing our strengths or challenging ourselves when something goes wrong. I believe God equipped all of us with a secret weapon to help us overcome so much more than we care to tackle when things go wrong, but we faithfully give up our will to live, although we say we trust in God, as we spend this quote on our dollar bills daily.

I really believed that I was going to be okay. Lying in bed one night, it seemed like my spirit would speak to me with instructions on how to get back on track. The instructions were not to depend on anyone, not to walk with a stick, and if at all possible, not to worry about anything! I knew in my mind that I was going to get through this. I had to learn how to do everything with my left hand and get out of the habit of trying to put both legs in the same pant leg at the same time. We never think that the small things really matter, like putting on that shirt and buckling that belt. It was all a challenge at this point in my life, but I didn't let this get next to me. This is life, and this is where I am this day. This too will pass, if I just stay focused. When I started trying to relearn how to drive, every day, I would sit in my car and try to understand the instrument panel. It took quite a while to really start understanding it and getting the confidence and the nerve to make an attempt to move my car any distance. I was fearful. It took years to get up the nerve to drive on the streets. One day, my sprit almost spoke out loud to me, "You can do this!" It had been almost five years since I had driven a car.

I was given specific instructions in my spirit to drive and the route to take. I was so afraid because I could not feel anything on my right side, and my vision wasn't that good. It was hard judging distance. I couldn't read signs, but I took it on. When I returned to my apartment complex, my legs were shaking so bad my brain took a while to register what I had just accomplished. I had not driven since May 1995. Here it was September 1999 before I really attempted to drive again. My brain kept reminding me that I wasn't ready for driving every day; that was just a test to let me know that I would be able to drive again, just not on the road right then. I started practicing every day in the parking lot by the complex where I was living. It was difficult, but I was ready for the task. I was not going to sit around depending on any one to teach me how to drive again, because they definitely would not have the patience they would need. Neither my right hand nor my right foot wanted to cooperate the way they should; plus, I could not read or understand signs that well.

In my condition, I didn't think anyone would have wanted to work with me at that time, trying to help me regain my driving skills. I was terrible. I didn't think there was enough patience available among the people I knew at that time in my life. I worked with the strength and the little knowledge I had left every day on my own. I wouldn't fail unless I gave up, and that was not in my DNA. Whatever it took, regardless of how long it took, I knew that I would drive again independently, with no one accompanying me. I would be victorious. I believe, at times, we are purposely tested as we journey through life. The stroke was a test of my faith, my strength, and my will to see if I could make it through this situation and stay focused. Life is a gift, and it's not free. The awesomeness of life is expressed through humankind. It is amazing. We are that human vehicle, traveling through this universe, not knowing when or if or life could be interrupted. We might feel misplaced, disgusted, and confused, but we must stay motivated and full of fire in order to succeed.

I am dealing with a life-changing illness. I am still here and paying close attention to everything. Sometimes, people would say certain things, and I really didn't understand, but I would act like I did. I would watch them intensely doing certain things. My brain was working overtime. I did not know how to do things in moderation. My mind and body would signal it wanted to relax, but I did not know how to stop and take a break. All the bodily processes that supported my mental activities were also going into a low-energy point when I didn't get my proper rest. I tried to recognize this natural recurring rhythm that went through my brain as I worked out daily. It took me a while to realize those moments when I would feel sluggish, mentally drained, and dull. I had to learn how to manage my brain power. It wasn't working at full capacity at this time, and I wanted everything right then, but I had to learn how to manage and not be so forceful in my condition. I had to learn how to stop and take a break. I did not understand I could not connect to a certain part of my brain.

For a long time, I wanted to feel and be normal again, but I did not know how to get there. Finally, I started getting it. I didn't think that I would experience anything ever again in my life that would be as devastating and as inspirational at the same time as this experience has been.

The attitude is key. I can't stress that enough. You have to fight for the right to live. Some days, I would get upset at myself because things were so hard to understand. One day, my spirit reminded me that life is only a repetition of things that I already knew. Patience would get me through. Life is a rerun, a repeat of the day before. Every day, we may do different things, but basically, we do the same things at the same times every day. When I really thought about it, I kept busy doing something as long as it wasn't something that would hurt me. I would keep going. I wanted to live and be independent, even though I didn't understand what I was doing the majority of the time. I kept busy at the risk of repetition. I began to get it right. That's just the way life is. When you think about it, life is a rerun from day to day every day. It's not easy, and sometimes, it gets harder as we proceed, but that's life. The first couple years after the stroke was the most difficult time of my life, but I keep going. I think that I am winning, even when the outcome seems to be proving me wrong. I am alive and living independently.

My thoughts and my focus are clear. Life is a journey, and this ride has been unbelievably amazing. I have never been afraid of failure, only not trying hard enough. I have never lost any of my passion or drive. Because of my circumstances, I taught myself discipline and I was persistent. I was always rewarded. I believed that if I pursued my recovery with passion, I would be anointed with the power to fulfill the mission and move on with my life. This has been an amazing adventure through life so far. I have ended up in the wrong places so many times through my recovery. I knew I wasn't where I wanted to be, and even being lost, I learned something helpful each time because of my willingness not to quit. It's those types of liabilities that became my greatest asset. They drove me. Even more, it strengthened my character every day. It gave me courage of an unbelievable magnitude. I was disoriented but fearless. Fear never entered my mind or my spirit during my recovery. I will be all right. When you are faced with a dilemma such as I was, to get through, remember, there is always something inside of you just waiting to be unleashed. It has to be a partnership with the creator. My liabilities made me desperate. It made me willing to do what so many aren't willing to do to get their lives back on track.

I have learned a lot about myself and my strengths. I have learned when I was down to nothing, God was up to something, but I had to be a willing participate as the human vehicle. My partner showed up to help put my life back together. The problem is that the thing that is so hard for me is the key to my promotion or success. There are so many things I could say to make that point, but I realize how important my liabilities can be. Without them, most of us would just settle for the status quo. I know life isn't easy, especially the situation I am in. Life is full of ups and downs, more downs than ups, and we are going to fall sometimes. Just know this: you can get up; you don't have to stay down. If you fall, try to land on your back. If you can look up, you can get up and get back on track. We should always send our words out in the direction we want to go. In other words, we need to always talk healing when we are down. We should talk about living when we feel like dying. We need to keep fighting when we feel like quitting. We need to keep moving when we want to stop. That's how I got back to where I am today. I still have a lot of work ahead of me, but nobody can do it for me, not even God and definitely not my kids. I have to believe that I can do this with God's help. Things happen in our lives, and we say we believe, but if things are too difficult, we quit. I knew that God was going to bless me through my situation. I said through the situation, we must stay encouraged and not only think of ourselves. I really didn't want to be in a home for the disabled. That was a lot of what strengthened me. If we just believe and don't faint, we can make it through so much more than we think we can. At our weakest, we are at our strongest. That's how we are designed. When you think you are at your lowest, you have been energized to conquer much more than you think possible. If you don't quit, life is an amazing teacher. Get to know yourself. Get to know your strength. That is your lifeline. Many of us are afraid to risk anything, but I had nothing to lose. I was already at my lowest point in life, except death.

A Letter from My Son, April 3, 1996, That Truly Inspired and Motivated Me

On April 3, 1996, almost one year after having the stroke, I received this letter from my youngest son, who was in the military. His words truly motivated me even more and bought me to tears. This was a few years after being able to somewhat read his letter with understanding, because I could not comprehend when I first received it. I did not alter one word.

Dear Dad,

How's everything going? Hopefully everything is going fine by the time you receive this letter. I've been thinking about you a lot lately but for some reason it's still kind of hard for me to pick up the phone, so I figured writing this letter would be easier. I know you're probably wondering why I haven't been keeping in touch. It is because I still haven't gotten comfortable with what happened to you. To me you were like this superhero type, you were like invincible to me. I never thought that I would ever see you in a vulnerable situation. I guess I never thought of you as being human. You're my father and you're supposed to be indestructible but then you had a stroke and it made me realize that you are human and because of that, you're vulnerable like everyone else. I can't begin to tell you how much seeing you lying in that hospital bed bothered me. It bothered me so much that the only way that I knew how to deal with it was to not deal with it. Seeing you in the hospital like that scared the hell out of me, it made me realize a lot of things. It made me realize that you weren't indestructible. It made me realize that you weren't this superhuman being with superhuman strength, which was and still is hard for me to come to grips with, but believe me I'm trying. Just to set the record straight, you are very important to me. It's because of you that I am the man that I am. You've always set the right examples and you've always been there when we needed you, and for that I am extremely grateful. The impact that you've had on my life is immeasurable and I don't know if I could ever repay you enough for that. All I know is that I can at least try and have the same kind of effect on my children as you did on me and if I'm lucky I'll turn my sons into men just like the one you are, the one that you made me. Well, I guess I'm finished with what I have to say, but before I go, I want to say THANK YOU for all you've done for me, for us. We all appreciate it very much, even if we don't always express it or seem ungrateful, and by the way, Dad, I love you.

Sincerely, Keenan

P.S. Happy belated BIRTHDAY.
I am sorry I missed it.

When I was able to read the letter from my son for myself with understanding, his words strengthened and motivated me in ways that I never imagined. I was even more determined not to give up. To accept failure as final is to be finally a failure. That's not me.

CHAPTER 4

GETTING BETTER
WITH TIME

It had been almost three years since the stroke, and I was still making progress, slowly but aggressively. I know this is going to be the fight of my life for the rest of my life, but I am seeing things a lot more clearly. Every day, I am feeling a lot more hopeful. I ask God each day to allow me to make this journey, and I truly believe that I will be granted that wish. Just a year or so ago, I did not know how to put that into words or if I would even be alive, but here I am, getting stronger and believing that I will overcome this challenge. My attitude has been key to my progress, that and not complaining about my situation.

Things are not as easy as they once were, but being alive, I have a chance to put my life back together. If it's God's will, I will just take one step at a time. I know I can beat this. I have been rewarded tremendously through my efforts so far, and no one thought that I would still be alive. Today, I took full advantage of the opportunity given to me, and I am so grateful and deeply indebted. I will not give up, and I hope I will be a beacon of light and encouragement for others. This journey has truly been a test and no joke. Sometimes, life overwhelms us, but we can't quit, even with all the ups and downs of life. I wouldn't trade them for anything. It only makes us stronger and more aware of what can happen to us on this journey.

Nothing stays the same. We have to adjust to life, and it's not that we have done anything so terribly wrong and we are being punished. Don't take it personally. That's life. At least I was given another chance or opportunity to see what I did with it. That's what I believe, and that gives me even more hope and strength. It also gives me a reason not to quit. There is no fail-proof blueprint on how to get through life without any battle scars. My children motivate me even more to do what I have to do to get my life back on track, and I hope I can encourage others through my personal efforts. My life does not have to be over because I had a stroke; I can make a complete recovery if I keep a winning spirit and want to recover. As a parent, I must do this. If they ever have to choose in an either-or situation, without hesitation, I would hope their faith will be great. Some of us will be tested, as we explore life, or does life explore us?

When we consider ourselves to be in a bad situation, maybe that's our faith being tested. That's how I personally feel in my spirit. If we always had everything good happen in our lives, then God would serve no purpose. He is in total control of everything, except our foolishness, and I believe His grace is sufficient for us, especially through difficult times. What that means is He has already given us what we need to overcome any circumstances we may encounter. I believe faith is a way of thinking, an attitude of mind that gets results. According to my belief, everyone has faith in something. Some have faith in failure or in sickness. When you hear exhortations to have faith, you must remember you already have faith. The question is do you know how to apply it to your situation or your life? Some of us will experience things in life or have been through something that we did not think we could overcome but did. At times, when we are down and depressed, we need to derive strength from optimistic thoughts. No one can ever unfold the mysteries of life. We just have to experience them as they come and hope that we don't get knocked out. Life is so wonderful, but it costs us at times in ways that are unimaginable. That's just life. I really hope that I have been an inspiration for the people that I have come into contact with while on this journey. It was very important to me that I regain my independence, especially for my children. I have to stay encouraged every day, even when I don't feel like it. It has not been easy tuning out distractions and self-defeating thoughts of dying without ever trying to win. Life is unpredictable and full of uncertainties. Every noble work is at first impossible, but we can do anything we want to if we get a plan and stick to it long enough. Your attitude is "Either I will find a way, or I will make one." Life is not always fair. Why do things happen like they do? I don't know; it's called life.

It's difficult and challenging all the time, but I had to hold on to my vision and my faith through all sorts of pain. Resentment is no way to approach life's challenges. I expect positive results in my recovery. I refuse not to find a way to stay positive, even when life sometimes seems cruel. I can't give up. My recovery requires lots of energy. That's just a natural response to a perceived attack or injury. I am improving my condition. I see myself on the other side of this situation. Every day, I have the victory already won, as long as I keep a positive attitude and keep believing and working toward my goal no matter how hard it might be. I was not too old to step out and be bold. I believed in myself and my capabilities. I kept my mind on the prize every day. My spirit told me I could make it. This was only a test. Sometimes, it takes devastating situations for one to tap into his or her God-given abilities. I keep going. I will not fail or falter; I will not weaken or tire. Neither the sudden shock of battle, nor the long-drawn trails of vigilance and exertion will wear me down. I have the tools, and I will finish this journey.

It's not easy, but I will make the pieces fit. I find it rather challenging, and it has definitely been rewarding. After a while, the ability to just keep moving is a job within itself. Every day, I tell myself, "You can do this. You were left here for this. If no one else believes in you, it's all right; you just don't stop believing in yourself and your vision of being independent again." I would say this to myself every day with authority, enthusiasm, and passion. As I worked on my rehab and as I moved forward, I was adamant, unyielding, and inflexible in will and purpose. "This is a piece of cake" was my saying. On the faces of others, I saw disbelief and antagonism when all the voices were telling me that I could not accomplish this goal. "You need to be in a home for disabled people," they would say. But my condition only strengthened, encouraged, and motivated me even more.

I believe that God kept me especially to fulfill this mission and to inspire others. Sometimes less is more. It is how you use it. I am determined to make a statement with what I have left. It is my responsibility to turn this into more. As long as I have the will, I will keep on living an independent life and continue encouraging others along the way. I will challenge myself. This has been the hardest and the most inspirational time of my life. I will persevere. If life starts to get harder, I will work harder and smarter, not lose my way and give up.

The real victory is already won in my mind and my spirit. There's no quitting or slaking off. I keep doing what has been put in my spirit. It's a feeling that will not be mistaken for any other. I feel like a winner every day. I am a winner, and that depends on me. As time goes on, I realize that a burden can become a passion and my passion can produce a new lease on my life. I believe I was chosen for this, and it has been one of the greatest life challenges that I could have ever experienced. I tried to set an example for my children through my experiences. When life gets hard, just a good enough attitude—just enough to get by—is not good enough. I have tried to leave a trail for others to follow so they can hold on to what they have left. No matter how hard it is, they should keep pushing. For a while, I wasn't able to let people know how much they encouraged me every day. I have come a long way. I never let myself get influenced by the few negative people I run into who say God might be strong enough to do anything but I don't think He's doing those kinds of things today. I say He still allows your healing, if you work for it. He will still deliver you if you want to be delivered. He will provide supernatural strength. He did for me. It is not outdated if you know how the word works. Your healing is tied up in you. You have to know this, and you must work for it.

He is still doing supernatural things like that today. I stopped going around negative people because I know that miraculous things are still happening in our lives today. If we stay positive and believe that it is possible, yes, even today, we can live by faith. It just has to happen to the right one. I know that those types of healings still exist today. I was created for this experience. I just had to maintain my faith, and that got me where I am today. This stroke has been so meaningful to me since I got to understand how God's word works through us if we let it.

I always work harder than the day before, looking to grow stronger. I am always seeking self-approval and hoping that I have been a dad that my kids can be proud of. They have kept me fighting to restore my life, my dignity, and my independence. I hope my fight has strengthened them for their journey through life, not knowing what lies ahead for them. The pathway of life is never predictable, but how we handle it can be. Take control. Your personal success depends on you. My attitude and my approach to life after the stroke told me what I could expect from life. If my nose is pointed up, I am taking off; if it is pointed down, I may be headed for a crash, so I keep my head up. That's one of the reasons why I have moved forward so gracefully. I challenged myself to do things every day that some doctors said I would not be able to do. Instead of lying around complaining, I had the right mind-set, and I always came out on top. I knew what I had to do after a while if I wanted to regain my independence.

I had to tackle my situation head-on. It seemed impossible to win this challenge at times, but fear would keep me disabled or kill me. My self-image meant everything to me. Self-image is the parameter to the construction of my attitude. If I don't put things back together, I will act in response to how I see myself and I will never get beyond the boundaries that the doctors and others had set for me. I am learning through my recovery, time after time again, that failures, repeated failures, are fingerprints on the road to achievement. It is impossible for me to succeed without some suffering. I didn't have to survive, but my attitude was the determining factor of whether I would make it or not. For me to accept failure as final is to be finally a failure, and that's not me.

Failure is the line of least persistence. I hate defeat, but that would have been the case if I gave up. I really don't think there's anything about me that says quit.

CHAPTER 5

STEPPING OUT ON FAITH TO RECLAIM MY INDEPENDENCE

1998

May 4, 1998, was the beginning of a real-life challenge for me, and no one thought that I would be able to overcome and put my life back together in an independent way. I moved into my own place exactly three years to the day after I had the stroke. I was afraid but determined to find out what I am truly made of. At the same time, I was fearless about what might be ahead of me. My spirit was never shaken. It was intact, but there were times when I wondered if I really would be able to live alone again. It was hard enough for me doing nothing and trying to understand the simplest things like locking my doors at night, closing my windows, cooking for myself without forgetting to turn off the stove, and running my bath without overflowing the tub, which did happen quite a few times and flooded my apartment. These were things that stayed on my mind constantly, but I still believed that I was left here for this reason. I will not give up. Sometimes, just thinking about where I was just a couple of years ago, I would get a headache. Things were even more difficult. I couldn't figure things out in my mind, but I didn't quit doing the simplest things I have done all my life. Living independently after a stroke seemed brand-new to me, but I had one of two choices: I could get busy living or lie down and die, depending on someone to take care of me. I chose to live. I thank God for the way He made me and the parents that I was raised by the short time I had them. It's because of them that I am not a quitter.

I could not wrap my head around that and call it living, ending up a vegetable or dead because of circumstances. Sometimes, we become bitter, depressed, and angry, but inside all of us, there is some amazing stuff. If we don't quit when things happen in our life, we will discover them. I say again, this just might be a test of my will. Wishing things were easier—that wasn't me and never would be. I have whatever it takes to recover if I am given the opportunity. I will not opt out because things are difficult or adversities rear their ugly heads. That is when my strength kicks in. I can't quit, but there were times when I wanted to. Sometimes, I knew what I wanted to do, but at times, I couldn't focus. I saw a passage written someplace that read that there are two times when you'll be the most vulnerable in life and want to quit; one is when you've suffered a great failure, and the second, believe it or not, is when you've just had a great success. The first one isn't a surprise, and the second one really isn't either if you think about it, because after you succeed, you can soon become complacent and forget who allowed you to make it through. That's why every day, I reminded myself of how blessed I am. I will never forget that things did not have to turn out this way for me, but I am eternally grateful in so many ways for how I have been allowed to deal with my situation so far.

My children have been instrumental in me maintaining strength to keep moving. I put myself in that position. When they were young, I used to tell them that as long as breath is in your body, you can overcome anything but death if you put your mind to it. I can't accept failure because of not trying, and they never forgot that saying and never let me forget it. Be careful what comes out of your mouth around your children; you might have to prove it to them one day. I had no other choice but to come through, no matter how hard it was. When they were young, they thought I was Superman anyway and that I could do or handle any situation. Believe me; that's where my drive comes from. My children have been the fuel that has kept this old human engine moving day after day, even when I didn't feel like it.

Maybe this will be a good read for them one day when they get older. They have truly been and still are my strength. I don't think that I could have accomplished as much as I have if I did not have them in my life. They make me feel like I had something to prove to them. I know that's not the case, but that's the way I feel inside and always will. When I started understanding my condition, I was convinced in my mind that I would make it. I have heard people say that they were so depressed when they were dealing with their situation, but I was always motivated through my children. I could not accept failure, not for a moment.

For a while, I felt embarrassed for people to see me in this condition, especially my kids. I could not walk right. I could not speak clearly. Directions were confusing. It was hard, but that did not stop me. I felt ashamed for people to see me like that, but it motivated me also. Even though I felt embarrassed at times, eventually, I overcame that. There was too much at stake, and every day, I could feel my strength being renewed in some way or another. I know this was a test. As Marvin Gaye said, I had to "get it on" at times. I didn't understand what was happening, but somehow,

I stayed focused and motivated. That was the key to me recovering. Sometimes, in our life, we say God will heal us while we are just lying around, even when we can get up and do something for ourselves. We must believe that all things are possible. Even in devastating times, we must try. We can't just give up. We can, but we shouldn't expect our healing without our participation. I believe that we all will be tested in some form or another before we exit this earth. If not, what was our purpose in the first place? Think about it; we are absolutely the most resilient specimens on earth, especially in the most difficult times.

I did not want to look back on my situation, my life, and wish that I had at least tried a little harder. I wanted to be able to say I gave it all that I had, no matter where I ended up, literally. We all have so much more strength than we think we do for the journey that's ahead of us. I made a commitment to myself. No matter how many times I fall, I will keep getting up until I can stand. Faith is one thing, but applying it is something totally different. Faith should not be taken lightly. It's more than just a word. It's life. It can move mountains with your cooperation. Trust yourself totally. You will be surprised what you can accomplish. I am finding out something new about myself every day through my faith. This has been an amazing journey.

My faithfulness has made it so, concerning my condition. The first mile of this journey was the hardest, making up my mind that I wanted to make the trip. The second mile was getting the first mile to register in my mind. I used up a lot of energy in the beginning, wondering what people were thinking had happened to me. In my condition, I know that might sound foolish, but for a while, that weighed heavily on my mind. I didn't want anyone to see me. They thought that I had a virus, but I let that go because I had a lot of hard work ahead of me. This was one of those times that as a man I would be measured by what I could accomplish through the opposition that I was faced with and the courage I maintained in my struggle for my life. I didn't want to look back on my life and see a lot of missed opportunities. I want to be able to say I did what some doctors said that I would not be able to do, but I am winning with God's grace and my willingness. I believe I am going to be all right. Since the stroke, I truly have given my best efforts every day and I have been rewarded. My spirit has been truly amazing on this journey, and my willingness to accept and work toward putting my life back on track in this situation really has strengthened me more than you could ever imagine. We must understand that sometimes difficult situations come our way. We just shrug our shoulders and don't try; we become angry and disgusted. I believe we must earn God's amazing promotions in life. We will if we just remain patient and faithful and do what's required. That's how I felt. From that time, I started to understand, but there was always that thought of no going back. I took control to the best of my ability with what I had left. I believe my destiny is in my hands to some extent. I didn't always understand that, but I stayed faithful to what I did know and that gave me huge rewards.

I know you might say that I am crazy for this next statement, but after the stroke has been the most inspirational time of my life. It has been so difficult but rewarding. I can't quit. Big moments seem to always come out of faithfulness in devastating times. I always do my best every day. I stayed motivated and kept going. I can do this. I know that I can. I believe sometimes we give up to soon. I sincerely believe that God chooses us at times. I believe this is an opportunity to test me, and I must stand up, step up, and use what is still available to me. I used to remind myself every day that this is just a test. "Lou, you can do this if you just trust and believe in yourself. Believe that you can." Believe me, you will if you want it. I know I was left here for a purpose other than to complain, but I had to believe that within myself.

I knew that I would make it before I did, because I felt it all through my body and in my spirit. It wasn't easy getting back to where I am today. I was given a mountain to climb or wear down so I could step across or walk around it. I have never been intimidated. I didn't get tired, well, not enough to quit. I was trying to save my life. If I didn't do my part in the natural world, God couldn't open doors for me on the supernatural side of life. I want to recover totally, and every day, I keep that in mind. As I journeyed on through life, I ignored the limitation that was put on me by the stroke and this disease.

It takes me longer to do things, but I am not limited to what I can do and I have nothing but time to get it done. I stay active. I find ways to enhance my life more every day. I want to live on my terms and live a life of accomplishments and not complaints about my condition. I want to live a normal life while still on this earth and not be under pressure. That can cause even more problems than the disease itself. They haven't found a cure, but somehow, they found ways to control the disease. For me, control has spelled cure to me. I feel good. I believe a miracle has happened in my situation already. I am still alive and have a winning attitude. That's 99 percent of the battle. I could see myself on the other side of this situation. My confidence is my vision, and my courage to rise above my situation is my destiny. I can't restore my future unless I keep a strong, focused mind. I do not spend time thinking about my loss or my problems. I ceased all negative thinking. If I had not, my mind would not function. Life is addition, said a tailor by trade. All he ever did was add. He never subtracted. He meant that prosperity is a plus sign. Add to your growth, wealth, power, knowledge, faith, and wisdom. I believe that the changes I have been through are a sure sign of God. The truth is that walking with God requires an ongoing, ever-changing experience. It is one of the sure signs that God is doing something in your life.

CHAPTER 6

ATTITUDE DETERMINES ALTITUDE

1999

Over the past few years, I have learned much about the amazing effect of the mind on the body and that has led me to believe that the majority of our healing comes from our mind, the internal monologue, or self-talk, and the resulting feelings, moods, and actions, as they relate to the body. Nutrition, exercise, and rest make a significant difference, as does a sense of belonging to a group of people, but most significant, for our purposes, is the exciting recognition by scientific medicine that people's attitudes, beliefs, and self-talk can make them sick or well or cause death. There are other factors in maintaining or regaining our health, but the mind has an important influence on improved physical health. The influence has often been neglected. How does this influence work?

We can gain insight into the mind-body connection by taking a careful look at one of the body systems most affected by positive and negative inner states: the immune system. Perhaps you've never had anything as significant and devastating as a stroke happen to you. It makes you look into all eras of your life. If you really want to regain your independence, you will find yourself trying anything you think will benefit you. At times, I did wonder whether I had enough left inside of me to overcome a stroke. That was the question that only God, myself, and hard work could answer. It depended on how badly I wanted to live. I continue to strive for 100 percent recovery. A few years have passed, and I feel good physically, but my motor inabilities on my right side challenge me every day. I am definitely getting stronger. I take my condition very seriously. The most important thing that I can do is maintain a winning spirit. It's hard, but I stay focused. That is the only logical choice I have if I want to keep living a productive, independent life. Sitting around feeling sorry for myself just won't get it done. I will be courageous and undismayed in facing the odds.

I will fight to overcome all physical handicaps and setbacks. I will try again and again and yet again to accomplish what I desire—all new faith and resolutions from the knowledge that all successful victims, men and women, have had to fight defeat and adversity. Life is a challenge, even when everything is going well. I don't allow myself to get caught up in failure conversation about how much work I have to do. Where I am this day is my reality, and the only thing that is going to get me through is positive thinking. This is life. This is the transition for the next part of my life.

That's what I believe. Nobody knows from day to day what the next second in life is going to be or what kind of situation one might experience. It took me a while to get it, but I am full of joy as much as my situation will allow at this time in my life. I would not have it any other way. I have really experienced some hard times, but I handled them well. That's the only way I could get back to some sense of normalcy for me. I am doing things that I never thought that I would be able to ever do again. I was unable to drive a vehicle for almost five years. I had to retrain my brain how to do everything. I would sit in my car for days on end and just look at the instrument panel until I started to understand it. I would not give up the physical and mental strength that I needed daily on this journey. It wore me out sometimes, but I kept a positive frame of mind and kept moving, even though things were very different and I had to find alternate ways of getting things done, not focusing on what I couldn't do. Eventually, I would get it back together. I remember when people were not able to understand me or I thought they didn't when I talked, but I did not let that discourage me.

I continued to try to relate. I watched TV, even though I didn't understand for a long time. I continued, and I practiced diligently on speaking clearly. It took a few years, but now, I am speaking much more clearly. Don't get me wrong; I still have difficulties with certain words, but like I said previously, I refused to defeat myself. I have thought about so many things while on this journey. I don't get discouraged. I just keep busy. I just take what's being given to me and build on it. I know this will be ongoing for the rest of my life, but I can handle this. What I can't handle is not trying. I have the rest of my life to deal with this. As long as I stay focused, I will make it. This is a piece of cake, considering the alternative.

I will not give up physically or mentally. My blessings could be in the midst of this. No one is exempt from things happening in life. Sometimes, your blessings can come through the most difficult situations, so still being alive overwhelms me. I just want to be in a position where I can take care of myself and show others through my effects that when you are faced with a life-changing issue, you don't have to give up living independently. My condition actually strengthens me every day, just knowing that I can fight another day. It makes me even stronger even though I am so weak. I kept thinking of someone else bathing me and preparing my meals. There is so much I would have given up, by putting the responsibility of my recovery in someone else's hands.

Life doesn't owe me anything. I owe life my contribution, and if I take it a day at a time, I can beat this. People always give me so much encouragement, listening and having conversation with them. When I could understand, they helped me with my healing process. I enjoyed conversing with people even though at times I didn't understand the conversation. I stayed right there and gave a nod of the head or something when I was out in public, especially when it was dark. My right hand wanted to lie across my chest, and at night, when I walked, when I approached someone, I would force my arm down by my side and swing it like I could use it, but I couldn't use anything on my right side. I couldn't even run if I had to. All I could do was fall to the ground. Have mercy on me, Lord. I know that I sound silly, but that was the truth.

No one knew how hard it was, not even myself, until much later. My senses were gone, but my spirit compensated. I was told how to handle things within in my spirit. I would listen when people would talk to me. I didn't understand for a long time. They didn't know, but they were a big part of my healing process. I just acted like I understood and looked serious. All I had to do was followed their lead, and it always turned out okay. When people joked, I did what everyone else did, and the joke could have been on me. It took me a long time to be able to relate with understanding, but no one else knew that and God. He wasn't telling that I couldn't comprehend. My sense of understanding is getting better slowly but surely. I like being around and interacting with people. That's the only way to regain self-confidence and some sense of what is going on around me. It helped me to rebuild trust. I was so fearful within my spirit. I had to get used to being around people again, but that calm I needed always showed up on time. I didn't understand it, but I know it was God protecting me.

I have been so blessed, and as time goes on, as God would have it, I started responding with some sense of understanding and clarity, but I knew that it would take years before I was totally confident of my interaction with people. Everyone I knew seemed like strangers, but I am getting there. You may think that the next statement I am about to make is trivial. Doing simple things like going into the store to pick up some milk and bread or any small items was like an act of Congress. At times, it has taken me all day to get a couple of items when I've gone into stores. I would be standing right beside what I wanted, but I couldn't identify the items. It would take a long time for my brain to connect, but eventually, it would come to me. Sometimes it would be so funny, but only through perseverance was I able to press on and endure the challenge of yet another hurtle. I continued to shop for myself, but it was no easy task. No matter how many times I went to the store, it was as though I was shopping for the first time. My brain will reteach itself at its own pace. I wish my children really knew the progress that I have made and will continue to make because of them. They strengthen me every day. I always showed the strong side of myself and gave the impression that I could do anything when they were around. I would never let them know how hard it was on this journey, and to this day, years later, they still have no idea how much of my recovery was because of them. I could not accept them seeing me fail. I felt obligated to set an example. I am still their father, and I can't quit because I know they are not exempt from something happening in their lives as they get older and live on their own. They may also be tested in some way, but today, they are my strength and my leaning pole when I am about to fall, if you know what I mean.

I hope that it's God's will for them to have the same inspiration, will, and tenacity that I have if they are ever faced with adversities in their lives. I am only here today by the grace of God and through my hard work and belief that I can rebuild my body and my mind. I know as I get older my brain power lessens, but I believe that it's still about my attitude, and I will find the strength to keep moving. I will get through this. Life knocked me down, but I didn't get knocked out and I definitely refused to walk and talk with them in the galleries of my mind on the belief that I couldn't make it. I practice walking the sunlit streets of my mind. When my life changed, I fought to stay encouraged and believed in myself and my hidden abilities and wonders.

I will make it. Faith is invisible and is the evidence of things not seen. I don't let the word *devastation* frighten me. I realize that I am a unique specimen created by God for a purpose and sometimes things happen purposefully to test our will, to see if we can make it through. If I don't receive another ounce of anything else pertaining to my health or my strength, I am okay. The writing of this book is to let others know that devastating situations can be your blessing in life, if you don't just lie there. If you can still look up, get up, and get busy with the faculties that you have left, they will rebuild themselves with your help. You can put your life back on track. You can have a productive life once again. But some people facing a setback like I suffered would allow themselves to just wither away, complaining and never attempting to explore the possibilities that they have within themselves.

This book is also to help you expand your inner strengths in a way you never imagined. You think you have lost it all, but you will be surprised by what you have left inside. Just don't stop living mentally, and your physical body can recover with your help. That's the way you are designed. Your attitude determines your altitude. Stay focused. Consciousness is the focused force of your will. Sometimes, things happen to us that are out of our control, but we have to play the hand dealt to us. It may be possible to make it a winning hand. You can be effective in others' lives again. I never allowed myself to feel burdened or angry with resentment because of my condition. It was a challenge for me. I wanted to make it even though things were difficult and incredibly hard. I knew that I was well-equipped for this challenge. We all have something special within us, and I believe that is why I received a second chance at life if I want it.

I was given the chance. It's my obligation to make a positive impact on my own and others' lives. When my spirit notified me that I had another chance at life, I took it even more seriously. The responsibility for my life became greater to me. We may not always be able to control what life puts on our plate, but I believe we can always control what we do with it after we get it. Just imagine looking back on your life as I have mine and discovering that you have used so few of your natural gifts because things got hard. A few years before I had the stroke, I started listening to tapes by Les Brown, and they made so much sense. We are the director, the producer, the scriptwriter, and the star of our own lives. We decide whether it's going to be a smash hit or a flop. It is in your hands. You are the master of your destiny. Anything is within your reach.

I believe in myself. It cannot be the end for my life unless I give up. There has got to be more; they say a quitter never wins and a winner never quits. Well, I guess they are talking about me. There is more, and I want my portion or my share. I know there is going to be even more tough times ahead on this journey as I attempt to put my life back together. I will fasten my mental seat belt and embrace whatever comes my way with a winning spirit. I can beat this, but it is going to be a bumpy ride ahead before I reach that comfortable zone. I will make it. Believe me, I must endure the turbulence of change in order to heal. I thank God every day for being so patient with me and allowing me to see my destination before I reach it. If you can't see where you want to go, you could end up anywhere. I approve of what I have accomplished so far, and I accept where I am. I love myself. I believe that I have done a good job thus far and have done all that I could have done in putting my life back together. I give myself approval and permission to move on as best I can. I am so grateful that I am still alive and in my right mind—well most of the time. It's wonderful. Always keep in mind that faith can move mountains, but fear can create some that you will not be able to climb. I had a hunger that developed a do-or-die attitude in me. I want to develop a habit of setting standards that my children and others will measure themselves by. I want to leave a trail for others to follow. I believed that I would be dead or seriously disabled, waiting to die or relying on someone to take care of me. I am so glad that God made me the way He did and I said yes to the invitation to live. I got up and got busy. Everything that I needed to make this journey was inside of me, but I knew I could not have made it on my natural strength. I always say that God is my partner. I felt inadequate for a long time and embarrassed by my situation until I started feeling and saying that God chose me for this mission. I really believe that. It took a while to get it, but better late than never.

I started giving maximum efforts to my recovery every day. We always expect something for nothing. While working a job, we are expected to produce. Listen to me, the difference between a highly successful person and an average person is those three words. No matter how hard I have to work, I am the one being directly rewarded so it was easy for me and I'm not just going to do what I'm expected to do. It's not fifty-fifty; it's all or nothing. I'm expected to do whatever it takes to get back. This is my life. I got a second chance to give my all, and I won't get talked out of my vision, which is independent living again. Life is a challenge, not only in difficult times; it's a challenge period.

That's not a complaint. It's just a fact. I am not a quitter. It's easy to wimp out, but that's not in my makeup. When things get hard, I work harder. I may never reach the mountaintop, but I will put so much pressure on the mountain that it will come down to my level if I don't quit, get complacent, or become discouraged. I have accomplished so much, but it's still no time to take that winner's lap. My recovery will be ongoing probably for the rest of my life, and I have no problem with that. It has been very difficult every day, and at the same time, my mind always stays clear enough to know what is still ahead of me concerning my situation. Everything seemed to be in place even when things looked dark, dreary, and different, but from my view, I kept fighting. I was allowed to see myself on the other side each day, so I didn't lose my way. I want to live and help others. I wish you could have known my dad. You would understand my drive. I can't give up because he wasn't a give-up kind of dad. I guess that's where I got my strength and my will. I feel like he is watching me every second of every day, and that's for real. I can't stop; this is another one of those crazy inserts that I can't explain, but that's how I feel every day.

My dad has been gone since July 1963 and my mom since September of 1978, and I can still feel their presence 24-7 since the stroke. I am representing them. They both are watching me. They have been my strength. They give me an overwhelming amount of courage. That's the kind of parents they were. When I am out walking or at the gym, they motivate me. They are always in my spirit. I know they'll never read this book physically, but I believe in my heart they have already read it even before I finish writing it. They put in my spirit to add certain inserts. I thank God every day that I am still alive and doing as well as I am, but they drive me 24-7. When I connect that with the strength I generate when thinking of them, my kids, and God's grace, I win. Believe me, that's what has carried me through this journey thus far. They keep me strong, forceful, and focused. That's where I got my strength from when I started to understand that I could make it back and when I became able to assess my condition. There were a thousand and one reasons to accept where I was with no fight, but they were my strength and my life. I couldn't let them down; they were in my spirit every day telling me, "You have the strength. You can get back if you keep the right attitude." That was in my spirit every day. We all are either the masters or the victims of our attitudes. It is a matter of personal choice. Because of the stroke, my life will probably be dedicated to helping others realize their strength or potential instead of settling into an unpopular way of thinking and accepting limitations that need not be placed upon them every day. Life is an ever-changing process of growth. I don't want to be in a wheelchair for the rest of my life. That's why I work doubly hard each day. I remind myself that this situation is for a purpose. It is not all about me. It is for others to learn and see what can materialize through me. I am nothing but a walking, talking human tool that God has placed on this earth for what I am going through this very moment.

I said before that I believe that I was chosen for this journey and I am afraid to give up or to quit. I have had some really hard days—I can say *years* with no exaggeration—but I knew in my spirit that God has kept me because He knew that I would be a beam of light. Others would see His work manifest through me. If not, what was the purpose? I want my life to be one that people will remember for the rest of their lives, especially what I came through with no complaints. I believe I was kept here for this journey, and that's why I work so hard. I always have something encouraging to say to people concerning my situation because no one knows if or when their life will change. As I said before, that is the mystery of life, and to me, that was a powerful enough reason for me to get up and fight back. Just being alive was not living. My biggest motivation was regaining my independence. That was number-one on my agenda. Life does not present us with a road map or the ideal situation, which will get us through life with no bruises. We have to motivate and inspire ourselves. I know now as difficult as it has been for me to go forward, it was more difficult to stand still and complain. I know that I have the capacity to overcome a lot more than I thought I could and lead a meaningful and productive life by awakening my consciousness as an active dimension of the human mind, not merely a passive vault where thoughts are stored.

Once activated, this consciousness becomes a driving life force to use for our betterment and the betterment of those around us. My condition has somewhat become a conversation piece because of what I have been through meeting and talking to people. It always gives me strength and a spiritual lift. There is so much strength in the right words. We are a lot more connected spiritually in our thoughts than we care to admit. When I was out exercising, people would motivate me in ways I never knew by something they would say about how dedicated I am to my recovery. It always gave me a huge lift. I seemed to get stronger immediately. It is amazing how sometimes the smallest things give me the biggest boost and the right words can make me feel so much stronger, depending on how they are formulated. There were times when I was exercising and I was so tired I could have passed out, but someone would say something that just energized me in such a way I could not explain at that moment. I felt renewed. It seemed as though there was always someone who gave me that spark I needed to do a little more that day, and I felt that they were there especially for me. I believe that's just how God works through us, depending on our faith in Him and ourselves when things happen in our lives. If we don't give ourselves a chance, God can't help us. There was something inside of me that reminded me every day how awesome I am, but at times, I really didn't feel like getting up and expressing that. Those were the days I worked the hardest. I definitely did not feel like exercising, but there was something that would not allow me to stop. I would go for a long walk, and while I was in that mode, all kinds of things would enter my spirit concerning my recovery, things like I would always work out when I didn't feel like it. When you feel energetic, take that day off to relax.

I didn't understand that for a long time, but it was so true. When I didn't feel like going to the gym or walking, those were the days I had to go exercise. We think that we are in total control. I beg to differ. I believe there are times we are faced with situations where we cannot get around certain things in life that have already been predetermined or put in motion before we existed. This statement is based on my belief. I never thought that I could be as peaceful as I have been coming through something so devastating. It truly has been a learning experience and the most educational experience of my life. What I feel on the inside is unexplainable. Everything that has come out of my mouth in this book has only touched the surface of what I really have been through. Some of it, I can't even put into words that would do it justice.

I've tried to explain to the best of my ability to give you some insight into how devastating this journey has been for me. Nothing has been easy, but I am not a quitter. Just keeping the faith has gotten me where I am today. At times, I've felt spiritually empty and physically broken, but I continued pushing forward. Sometimes when we get knocked down, it's only a test. I truly understand that since the stroke. I could not have made this journey on my own strength. I would not be writing this book if I had chosen to live in the safe zone after the stroke. God couldn't have used me for others to see His awesomeness at work in me. I could not have felt His promise for me every day if I had stayed in the safe zone, lying in bed day after day, complaining, not trying, waiting on God to heal me with no input on my part. I would not be here. I had to get up no matter how many times I would fall, and when I convinced God that I was ready to do what I had to do, then He allowed me to go even further forward with my healing. It wasn't easy, but I believe that's the only reason I am still here today.

CHAPTER 7

RECONNECTING TO THE WORLD I ONCE KNEW

2000

Every day, I am getting stronger and stronger in so many ways. My focus has gotten so much better. I am reclaiming and reestablishing the quality or state of being independent again. I am still living on my own, but there are so many things that are still not clear to me or I don't really understand. I still get confused, but I don't let it get me down. I can feel myself gaining momentum, and it feels good. It's not easy staying motivated. I have to work extra hard to keep myself focused. It is a heck of a challenge. My retribution and my rewards depend on how I use my mind. I still believe that I was chosen for this mission or test for the purpose of helping others. Within all of us is that conquering spirit waiting to be activated if we chose to act. Sometimes, we defeat ourselves by complaining. We say we have faith, but faith is action. We are still not guaranteed to win, but a try beats a failure any day. Our entire lives are built on our faith. We should feed our faith every day, walking by faith into the unknown territories of life. In my case, I know I was given this challenge to overcome. I believed I had what it would take to regain my independence, but I still get confused at times on how to proceed day by day. It's not easy trying to reconnect or reclaim misplaced pieces of my life and move on. It's really difficult trying to make sense of it at times. But I accept where I am and how my life has been unfolding physically and mentally. I try to rise up a little higher each day, and the battle goes on. I find out a little more every day about myself. I knew that faith alone was not going to be enough to get me back from this unfamiliar place. I was being tested daily. Things seemed so foreign; sometimes, I would spend days just trying to figure things out before I could proceed. I was in the fifth year of my recovery, but at times, it felt like it was just beginning. I had been living on my own now since May 1998. It was very difficult, but as time went on, I seemed to be getting better at handling my situation. I didn't wear myself out or become so drained by the end of each day anymore. I became more patient, which I had to do if I wanted to continue living on my own. I am determined to manage that inner climate. I feel it is so close, waiting for me to take back control of my life totally. There is nothing like that feeling, and nobody can fill that void for me but, so I took responsibility. It has been rewarding. I never worry about anything pertaining to my condition because I am where I am with what I have to work with, so why worry? That would only cause me more stress and complications.

I am learning so much from my condition. I am becoming more patient. I am in a place that I never thought that I would be in life, but I am at peace with myself. I have been given something within my spirit to be able to handle this, and I hope that I will strengthen others I come in contact with or who read this book. I have tried to the best of my abilities to put into words what I have gone through from the beginning of this journey. I feel so privileged to have been chosen for this. That may sound crazy, but that's how I feel. I can't explain it. I can't put it into words beyond what I have said already. I have never felt such calmness as I have since I have learned how to handle my condition. I have been so peaceful within, and I believe all of us have that inner strength and that capability when things happen, if we just step back a moment. It takes a strong will with a very determined mind to reach it in devastating times that are so overwhelming.

I press forward, forgetting what happened to me. I keep my mind on what I want to accomplish. It hasn't been easy, but with God's grace and the right attitude, I will make it a day at a time. I have really found joy in the midst. This has been the test of my life, and I believe and trust that I will get through. At first, I thought it was impossible. There were times when I was in a battle in my mind because things that I was going through didn't seem to be beatable. I would find myself trying to correct things that were already in place, but they seemed wrong to me. I was so confused, but as time permitted, I would start understanding that things weren't wrong. It was me.

A little at a time, I started to understand that the way things seemed to me were false, so I kept pushing forward. I have enjoyed the ride. I've learned to depend on God as never before. I can tell you from my own experience that when your brain is affected and you find yourself experiencing things that seem to be beyond your ability, trust and believe. Put it in God's hands, and leave it alone, but be ready to do your part. The things that are within your reach are your responsibility. Stay focused. You will make it. Keep reaching up and grabbing hold, and hold on like never before until something materializes. That's what I call faith. It does not matter how much religious activity is going on in your life—if you are not relying on faith, you won't make it.

Because it is the pathway to success and you must give your all until you succeed.

Life is only yours for a moment, so when you are in that moment, give it everything you've got with all sincerity, never doubting yourself or your mental and physical abilities. You must work hard. Don't get discouraged. Believe in God. You have everything you need just waiting on you. I feel that I have a purpose. I will keep on trying to encourage others to the best of my ability through my recovery. This has been the most inspirational situation that I have ever been in in my life—and the hardest—but I stay focused and keep my eyes on the prize. That is for total healing. I believe that when God saw the passion that I brought forth in my recovery, He released something extra for me because of the overwhelming passion that I accept every day.

I read someplace that power follows passion, so when my passion grew, it gave me awesome powers. I needed them to accomplish my God-given purpose. I asked for guidance, and it was always granted. I was willing to take risks for my life and try new things. My spirit let me know a lot about myself on this journey. Sometimes, my answers didn't come right away, and it was the opposite of what I thought, but it would always come on time. Every day, in my mind, I thought He just might be testing my will today, but I will always be willing to go into unfamiliar territory. He has supplied me with everything I have needed, and I will not stop now. I have come too far, and I know things can still happen, just because that's life; what I will do under those circumstances is stay focused and move on.

Faith is where miracles happen. Sometimes, I feel like I am losing the battle, but all through this book, I am winning the war. I keep talking about the test of the human will. It gives life. The only way to turn negatives into something positive is to win the war. Sometimes, you can experience serious setbacks, and depending on the type of person you are, you can come back, but staying connected to that winning spirit is key. That was my vehicle to recovery.

As I was healing, I could see myself on the other side of my condition daily. You must keep a clear vision of what you want to accomplish. If not, you could end up anywhere. Listen to your spirit. Do the right thing. You will not be guided wrong. My mind was so out of tune with reality for a few years, but no one else knew from the way I handled myself. Somehow, some way, I made it back. Sometimes, I think about where I was in that period and where I am today. It is absolutely amazing. Some days are amazing. Many days, I have cried like a baby just thinking about how blessed I have been on this journey.

Many times, I wanted to give up, but in my mind, there was something that would not allow me to do so. I could hear something at times. When you are right on the edge of a breakthrough and you want to quit, instead of turning back, you need to say to yourself, "I am too close to quit now." Don't get discouraged. You are getting close to something. The greatest weapon I have while recovering is my mind, and I am a winner. I am a survivor.

I have never been discouraged, concerning my condition. It motivates me. I have never even thought, *Why me?* I have always said that I was chosen for this journey. I guess it was because I looked at it as a blessing. I was in a coma, but I made it back, and I am still here. I have maintained a winning spirit. Life is an adventure, a test of the human will. That is why I held on tenaciously. I believe the universe will be kind and on your side. It has been proven in my case. I know within myself, while I am fighting for my life, that sooner or later, the wheels are going to turn my way. I can feel it because I was working so hard, and somehow, I believed that if I endured and persevered, I would position myself to overcome and succeed.

Sometimes, we can be forced to spend time looking at life from a different perspective because of our situation. It's not always because of anything we have done or are doing wrong. That's just life. In hard times, we must hold on. Life is an adventure, and we must be adventurous as we journey through this universe. Whatever we may be going through, whatever the reason may be, there is always that possibility that you can make it. I used to tell myself this every day, and at the same time, I work hard for what I want to accomplish. Without my independence, what good is life? Maybe one day, I will try to get into motivational speaking, if only to let people know how inspirational this journey has been for me.

If I had dwelled on the discomfort and pain—having no vision in my right eye and no sense of direction, being unable to hear, my mouth feeling like it was in the wrong place, and so many other things—I would not have made it, so I kept myself busy enough to not have the time to worry or think about my limitations or my overall condition. Honestly, I really did not understand for a while how to put the pieces back together, but as time would permit, I got it right or I am getting better. This has been the greatest and the hardest experience of my life, and yet it has been so inspirational.

Lupus is only a condition. Life is an experience that can and will get me through this journey. Sometimes, I would like to just stop all the medications that I am taking. It does get on one's nerves, always trying to remember whether I took my meds today or yesterday, but I have to keep in mind why I am taking these meds. That's when everything becomes very clear to me. I will be taking these meds for the rest of my life, and it became a lot easier to remember not to let my meds run out. They really are my lifeline, along with plenty of exercise, eating the right foods, and staying out of the hot sun as much as possible. My meds, eating right, and exercise are my first love and my main priority; they override everything else, and I don't forget my refills anymore. When this first happened to me, I couldn't remember to take my meds. They were my strength in a bottle, and I didn't know what could happen to me on this journey through life.

I believe that when this happened to me and I was left here, it was my duty to bring forth the best I had to offer myself and to encourage others along the way. No matter what happened to me, I still had some life left in me. My attitude concerning my situation can be seen without a word being said. Sometimes, the attitude can be masked outwardly, and others who see us are fooled, but not making an effort in my situation, I am only robbing myself. In the situation that I am in, it is my responsibility to put my best God-given efforts to work. I make it my business to try to relocate the greatness within me. It is important that each day, I try to reach a new height. When things happen in our lives, some of us never exert ourselves to move up and grab hold of God's provisions. I believe that's reserved for us; instead, we complain ourselves into a deeper hole. If we don't try, we'll never know the importance and significance that our situation has in our life. Most of the time, all our good stuff is still left within, but we have to reach for it. We must want it badly. It won't be easy to put your life back together. For me, this has been a challenge and a chance to inspire so many others, especially my children. When people say it's over for you, it can be the start of a new beginning at life. It is up to God. If He says yes and keeps blessing me, who else matters? From that point on, it is up to me to do the rest. I try to use my condition to inspire people, and that keeps me motivated even more every day. Your problem can be the key to your motivation and your promotion in life. It's up to you to make the connection. I have learned that when you are down to nothing, if you stay focused, God can do more for you. You have to believe and trust Him. For me, it has been proven throughout the last seventeen years of my life.

I have had some hard days, but complaining would have only made things worse, so I always kept my head up through my ordeal. Good things have happened for me because of my attitude. Every morning, I got up early and worked hard all day. I was so grateful for having such a thankful spirit. It was always at a high level, no matter how I felt physically. Many days, I would walk in the snow and the rain just to get strength. It was so hard, and it was so cold, but I would make the trip. It was exciting for me, regardless of the weather. It was a must. I didn't complain, and it always took me to another level in my recovery. In my mind, things were not easy. I knew I was going make it. There was that reminder again. It has been all about my attitude, and it continues to be. I feel that I can walk across water and won't go under. My attitude is my lifeline. It's what has kept me alive, but how good I do physically is my choice. I always maintained a winning spirit, even when I didn't feel like it. I do what's required of me. This adventure has been well worth it for me, even more so when things were tougher. Who am I, and what am I really made of? I have to ask myself these questions. Many times, because I am so focused on regaining my strength level, this has been the highlight of my life in every way you can imagine because I kept the faith.

I always saw myself on the other side of this situation. I didn't sweat it, even when at times recovery seemed impossible and I had no answer. I stayed cool, and my spirit would remind me, *You are still alive. You are in charge. You can make it back. Just don't give up.* I stayed committed every day to the things that I was allowed to do. I never had to force myself to work out. My natural instinct just took over. When I thought of someone else having to take care of me, I gained strength, and things got easier.

Many people perceive difficult times as a time to stop living and barely exist instead of taking a positive stand and viewing the difficult times as an opportunity to find out what they are made of. That may be the place and time for the experience of your life. Every day, when I get up, I thank God for giving me another shot at life and keeping me in such a position to place in my mind and to have a fighting chance to come back if granted the opportunity. I am going to make it. My saying every day is, "I'm doing better than good, and better than most in this devastating situation, sometimes even better than that."

I am at peace with myself. I embrace my situation. I embrace good health. I embrace everything good in the universe. During my recovery, I tried to seek out people who empowered me, people who inspired me, people who encouraged and complemented me, people who always knew what to say to me. When you are going through hard times, even feeling depressed or down, you have to stay mentally strong. That helps you overcome the downside of life. It took an enormous amount of energy to reach where I am today, and it will take even more to move on. I am striving continuously to further my recovery, going to the gym almost every day. This is my life, and only God's grace makes it possible for me to stay strong. I know He is my strength, and I am afraid to complain. I will not lose sight of who really allows me to still be here and helps me through this dilemma. I say thanks so many times during the day for God allowing me another opportunity at life.

When you are down, becoming an optimist is easier said than done, but I learned to notice the more positive side of my situation, though I was going through hard times. I wanted others to see how I handled my recovery. Believe me, it really is all about His creation. In the United States, we say we trust and believe in God; we read our Bible, we go to service, and we pray, but when things happen in our lives, do we really trust God? The stroke has been so inspirational for me. This has been the most amazing time of my life. I can't put into words the way I really feel inside. You just have to believe me. When I go out to do my daily walk and exercises, there is always such a calmness in my spirit. The exercises are hard, but they feel light on my soul, like someone is guiding me and lifting all the weight off me. When I was told by the doctors that I had to have a wheelchair and possibly use a walking cane for the rest of my life, I said okay, but I had already been notified in my spirit that I wouldn't need it unless I wanted it. When I returned home from the hospital and rehab, my tub would have to be modified so I would be able to pull up after taking a bath. I was told many things would have to be modified because of my disability and I possibly would still end up in a home as time went on because I would not be able to live alone. That was some of the doctor's advice, but with God's help, we proved them all wrong. It was all about my attitude, which is my life. I learned how to reinvent myself and the circumstances I want in life. This was nothing but a temporary setback, testing my will to make a comeback.

The interruption in my life was only to test me and my qualifications before I exit this earth for my final destination. Only by His grace, I was granted a few more days to bless others with my life. I said somewhere earlier that living in the faith zone, when things happen, you have to reach up and grab hold of nothing and hold on to it until it becomes something. I knew God wanted me to live. I could feel it in my spirit; that was why I couldn't give up and lay around complaining. I was obligated to keep moving, even when my body was saying no. There was something inside, challenging me every day to stay faithful and willing. I would make it. Life is a temporary gift. We don't know how or when it could be over. I had nothing to lose. I stretched myself again and again. I couldn't stay in the safe zone. There was nothing to gain. I needed to put it all on the line if I wanted to live and be where I could help others to see that life is not always over even when it seems like it is. That's where the miracles kick in. I would have never made it if I had stayed in the safe zone. When I started taking risks, I started regaining my strength. I had to listen to the Holy Spirit as I knew it and release my fears. I believe I can make this journey. I asked God to help my unbelief, fill me with courage, and furnish me with faith. I had to keep feeding my spirit every day.

I am a man who possesses a strong faith, but sometimes life can catch you off guard. Believing and trusting that an overshadowing providence is always watching over me, I am kept away from unpleasant experiences that might harm or injure me in some manner. Just like oil and water repel one another, my faith in God and His love and the unpleasant experience repel one another according to the law of belief.

CHAPTER 8

CONTINUAL PROGRESS

2001

I named this chapter "Continual Progress" because that is what the rest of my life is going to be about, strengthening and regaining my independence. I know that I may not ever get back to 100 percent, but I am sure going to try my best to get as close as I possibly can. In this stage of my life, I know that I have to work smarter not harder. That means I have to keep trying even when there seems to be no hope. I have to keep working even when I am tired and feel like quitting. I have to encourage myself to keep going. Life is a gift, and I have to keep on giving even at times when I feel like I am getting no return. I am always surprised when I feel like there's nothing left to give or when I feel like I am on empty.

I believe God preserved my life to help others, and this has given me a purpose for living. I don't know what that purpose is at this moment, but I do know the way I have handled this situation was His reason for leaving me here. Like the song says, "It feels good." There's something in my spirit that feels mighty good. I refuse to accept my diagnosis as a death sentence. I resolve, with your help, to make this diagnosis an occasion to refresh, renew, and strengthen myself and others, so that they believe in themselves. In my conquest of illness and death, life is not easy all the time. It will test you, not because of wrongdoing but just because that's life, so I continue to be grateful and reach deeper and deeper inside of myself daily to try to put the pieces back together, encouraging others while on my way. I can't change what has happened by complaining, but I definitely can be mindful of how I handle the situation. I am always amazed at how quickly people give up on themselves when something happens in their life. Hardship is a part of living. By saying, "Why did this happen to me?" most of us act as if we were born with the great expectation that life was going to be easy and if we do the right thing, everything will work out the way it should or the way we want it to. There is no need to panic. This is life, so get prepared to handle it without personalizing it.

We are capable of enduring life's most difficult challenges. I am reminded almost every day that I am alive. I believe that the human spirit has the capacity to overcome even something more devastating than what I am going through at this moment. I stay encouraged. I talk to myself. At times, I ask myself questions and answer them. I do anything that I think will help me. I use it as long as I know that I will keep making progress, but for a long time, my surroundings seemed so unfamiliar, it felt like I had never been there before, but as I try to find my way back to the world that I once knew, where I am now, this day, it sure feels great. The price was high, but the rewards have been worth the trip. I probably will never come to the end of this on this journey, so I will continue enjoying the ride.

This is from a quote I saw somewhere: the biggest room in your brain had better be reserved for things you don't understand. If you have to understand everything before you will trust and believe in God, you don't understand the concept of faith! If you think just because you are in the will of God, everything will be good and you won't have any stormy times in your life, you really don't understand the word. I don't presume to be a biblical scholar in the writing of this book; I am just voicing my opinion about things that I believe and have experienced on my journey. I could be wrong about my opinions, but that is how I feel. As long as I am doing as well as I am, I will continue on this path. Everybody's journey through life is different, but the end result is the same. So give it all you've got on your way through and be happy. Life is not always fair, and it is unrealistic to think that it will ever be as long as you are alive. Never quit; you will succeed.

I always knew that I was going to make it because I was born a winner. I will not allow my circumstances to shape my future and destroy my self-image. I am determined to make it no matter how hard I have to work. Even a temporary give-up can end my life. My conscious mind reminds me of that. Every day, life is an experience. We only get one chance to make a serious impression, and this is mine. I am not going to let life slip away without a fight. I will make it. The choice is mine. Every day, my spirit lifted me a little higher. My attitude is the difference between being successful and being a failure. I will succeed. I don't have any doubt in my mind.

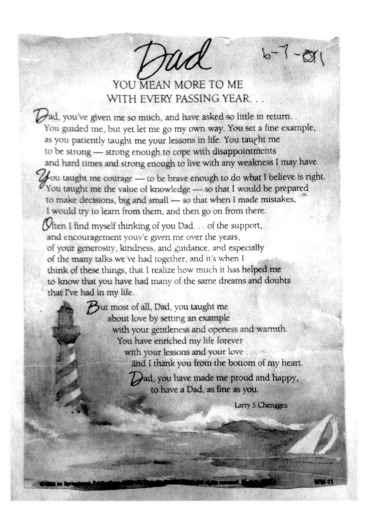

Dad 6-7-01

YOU MEAN MORE TO ME
WITH EVERY PASSING YEAR. . .

Dad, you've given me so much, and have asked so little in return.
You guided me, but yet let me go my own way. You set a fine example,
as you patiently taught me your lessons in life. You taught me
to be strong — strong enough to cope with disappointments
and hard times and strong enough to live with any weakness I may have.

You taught me courage — to be brave enough to do what I believe is right.
You taught me the value of knowledge — so that I would be prepared
to make decisions, big and small — so that when I made mistakes,
I would try to learn from them, and then go on from there.

Often I find myself thinking of you Dad. . . of the support,
and encouragement youv'e given me over the years,
of your generosity, kindness, and guidance, and especially
of the many talks we've had together, and it's when I
think of these things, that I realize how much it has helped me
to know that you have had many of the same dreams and doubts
that I've had in my life.

But most of all, Dad, you taught me
about love by setting an example
with your gentleness and openess and warmth.
You have enriched my life forever
with your lessons and your love . . .
and I thank you from the bottom of my heart.
Dad, you have made me proud and happy,
to have a Dad, as fine as you.

Larry S. Chengges

From my daughter Kelly 6/7/01 after
the stroke, love you Dad

CHAPTER 9

RELOCATING AND CONQUERING NEW CHALLENGES

2002–2003

On March 30, 2002, I relocated from New Jersey to Birmingham, Alabama, to live with my sister for a while. It had been seven years since the stroke. I thought the transition to new surroundings and a different atmosphere would contribute to my recovery process. I don't want to just get better; I want to gain mastery over or win by overcoming obstacles or opposition that no one gave me a chance to overcome. My sister owns a single-family home, and it has a completely finished basement at ground level. That was good for me. It would be my home for a while.

My next priority was finding a reliable personal physician. A few weeks after arriving, I had to see a doctor concerning my condition. I chose Princeton Hospital. Dr. Willie William Jr. was the first physician I saw after my arrival. On my first visit, I knew that he would be my primary doctor. I liked his personality. He was already a physician at that hospital. We hit it off immediately, and he has been my doctor now for a little over ten years. I could not have located a better physician/friend. He is always there for me whenever and for whatever if I reach out to him. I know he is going to reach me shortly. I thank God for placing him in my path. We get along so well.

The transition was good for me. I liked where I was living, and I enjoyed working in my sister's yard, cutting grass, trimming hedges, and doing anything I thought would help my recovery. I really liked where she was located. Everything was very convenient for my condition. There were no steps to climb if I didn't want to. I loved it. The basement had no stairs from outside. It was perfect for me at that time in my recovery. I only stayed there about a year and a half, but it kept me busy and my mind occupied. My sister had a dog named Fatboy, and he was my buddy and another source of daily exercise. He was fun and so active. That was excellent physical therapy for me. I wanted to get back to living on my own, being independent, and making my own decisions in my own place. In August 2004, I applied for an apartment, and on September 4, 2004, I was finally moving into my own place to live alone. I was excited and afraid at the same time. All kinds of thoughts were running through my mind, because everything was so different from what I was used to, including the landscape. There were no sidewalks. I had to readjust to everything. I wasn't ready for this, but I was finally living on my own. I lived there for approximately seven months. I had fallen on the stairs a number of times, but I escaped injuries each time. That was my cue to move to something more suitable for my condition.

I was allowed to break my lease early with no penalty. I moved to Forest Ridge Apartments, where I am still presently residing. This place fits my condition quite well. I am on the first floor in the front. I am near the office, and management is always there for me. I could not have found a better place to live. This place has served me very well. Sometimes, I feel like God went ahead of me, preparing things for me, and I say this sincerely; all through my recovery, everything has seemed to always fall into place at the right time. My transitions have worked out so well for me. I truly understand what we mean when we use the expression *stepping out on faith*. This has been a faith transition, living on my own in a new city after having had a stroke.

This was a mysterious, exciting, complicated wonder. My mind was getting some clarity and letting me know I could do this. My faith had come full circle. It was the key since having the stroke. I never understood how our faith really works until I had the stroke. Everything I need to recover is already inside of me. I am learning that faith can only work for me if I believe and am willing to step out and claim it. I believe my life was being tested when I moved here to Alabama. That was really on my mind every day. I was wondering whether this transition would be good for me because of my condition. Could I make it here? However, I was assured in my spirit. I know that God is using me every day, and I am grateful. Life was God's gift to me, and not giving up is my gift to God.

His power works here the same as it does in Jersey. We have to stop putting limits on God and ourselves. I can do this, if this is where I choose to live. I had to stop restricting God and myself. I will be okay. After a little struggle within myself, things have changed tremendously. I believe some things we go through in life are just because that's life, and some things are predestined and we can't get around them. My faith in God has gotten me where I am today, and it will carry me on. I was given instructions on how to use my secret weapon that I've had since birth on this journey. That weapon is my willingness to overcome what I am faced with, and it is inside, waiting on me. Most of us complain so much we kill it.

We give up, and we never recover. I will not be one of those people, wondering if I could have made it if I had only tried. What good is being alive if you show no willingness to live? I have a productive life again since I relocated to Alabama. There was another hurdle surrounding me: meeting new people. The landscape was totally different from what I was used to. It is all about the human spirit and a willing mind. I was ready for change. I was looking forward to new challenges and new surroundings. It would only strengthen me. I would overcome, and this would be a measuring tool that others could use one day. It is another piece of life's amazing puzzle.

I have much more living to do. When I realized the situation that I was in, it seemed like all the odds were against me, but I kept a good spirit and definitely a winning attitude. I had been kept here for a reason. How I handled it was up to me. Life with this disease is deadly, but I am determined. We were made for each other. I know that I might give out, but I won't give up as long as I am breathing. I feel an elevation in my spirit, and I see a change in my condition every day. Life is all about attitude, and I have that. I will make it here. Alabama's summer seems twice as hot as Jersey's, so I have to be twice as smart and a lot more cautious when I am out doing my workout. This is just another part of this amazing journey that's called *life*.

We were given a brain to figure some things out for ourselves, and I really try to exhaust everything that's available to me, pertaining to regaining my health. There is so much that I didn't say in this book concerning my journey through my recovery, but remember this; when things happen in your life, expect to get positive results.

We have to work for them every day, and sometimes we overlook that fact. That's why we were put here in the first place. Sometimes, things just happen and we haven't done anything wrong. It's called life. I feel kind of special that I was chosen for my situation. I believe we all have those special God-given talents within us. We don't care to have to use them, but we must. If it's not your time to exit, you are not going anywhere. Believe that, and get busy, but you have to want it.

For me, this has been an amazing journey and the most spectacular experience of my life. My condition keeps me encouraged more than you will ever know. I want to keep living and not just barely getting by. My belief creates my thoughts. My thoughts generate feelings, and my feelings affect my body's healing systems. So many thoughts prepared me for my healing and where I am today. I have learned how to align my life, my goals, and my actions so that I have the most congruent life plan and learn how to dissolve challenges, overcome obstacles, and manage my emotions concerning my situation. I can choose to maintain a positive attitude or just settle, but the challenge has been awesome. I keep moving forward and staying positive. I will get back. I was not left here just to complain to everyone I meet on this journey.

I put my faith in the right place. I put it in God's hands while doing my work. He is the only one who knows what I can get through. We can only imagine. I am living proof. From my own personal experiences, I know that if I believe and don't quit, my inner strength always amazes me, so when you think that you have nothing left to work with, believe me, you are mistaken. That's why you were given a brain. Use it. Figure it out. I know I have made this statement many times over, but I was told by many doctors that I would never be able to live on my own again and definitely not be able to drive anymore. They said I would have to use a wheelchair and would have to be in a home for the disabled, but they were not going to dictate to me the kind of lifestyle that I would have. God is the author of this universe. I didn't know what to do when I first got here. The bus system wasn't that good. Certain areas had no bus at all, but this is where I chose to move, so I had to accept the services that were available and move on. I can't change the system, but I can change me.

CHAPTER 10

GETTING BACK
ON TRACK

This journey has been threatening, challenging, but mostly fulfilling for me. I have learned so much about the human spirit and the human will, as well as the ups and downs of life, in the struggle to regain my independence and maintain my dignity after having a stroke. When I first started to really understand and see things a little more clearly, the first thought in my mind was, *Do you really think that you have what it takes to get back to independent living?* This was followed by, *Do you really think you have the patience required to overcome such a devastating situation? When things get hard, will you have the courage to keep going and not give up?* "I can do this," was my response.

I find this journey to be very therapeutic. I am learning so much about myself, being knocked down at my age. The changes I have to make every day challenge me. It will not be easy. I remember when I first started on this journey and I was trying to relearn how to exercise again. It was no joke. I thought I wouldn't make it. I had no balance. I was clueless as to what I was doing. Some people thought that I was on drugs or drunk, and I didn't know what to say. I had lost so much weight, and that contributed to being off balance. I had never heard of this disease. I had no idea what to expect or how it would affect me and change my life forever.

I did not know the severity of this disease, but I learned quickly how my life would be impacted. Everything around me seemed to change. All the odds seemed to be against me, but I kept a winning spirit and a willing attitude. Every so often, the thought, *What if you can't beat this?* entered my mind. *What if you fall flat on your face? What if you make a fool of yourself?* There was no stopping me. I had nothing to lose because I had seemingly lost everything already. What was the risk, other than regaining some of what I had lost or being stuck where I was? I never tired. That was not going to happen to me. God willing, I will win this fight and regain my independence. This disease is deadly, and I also find it exasperating in hot weather, but I try my best to live as normal a life as possible. If I sit around dwelling on my condition, I will be miserable. That's why I keep busy. I am feeling great. I refuse to see things any other way because life is only right now, this moment. I try to stay in the moment as much as I possibly can, and I always keep in mind that even in the best of health, we are only here for a moment and things will happen to us on this journey called life. Things change. There is nothing we can do about it. There are only three guarantees in life: taxes, death, and trouble. I try to stay out of trouble, pay my taxes, and thank God for the start of another day. I enjoy my life to the best of my ability.

I am always reminded that life is on loan. It's a gift, and I have learned to enjoy it while it lasts. I got a second shot, so I give it my best this moment. If by chance tomorrow is granted, I do a repeat of yesterday and today and stay focused. That's all I can do. My mind is always in a positive and peaceful place at all times—well, most of the time. It's not easy, but it is possible. Therapeutic thinking is the key. It has a beneficial effect on my mental state in serving to relax and calm my spirit. It also helps me in restoring my physical strength, which is still having a tremendous effect on my recovery, but the joys of life are worth the struggles.

I must maintain my patience and engage in persistent action every day while regaining my independent status. I won't give up so easily. I won't give up at all. I've found a different kind of strength in this life, treating my struggles. I am my own motivator because I love life and I love myself. I don't depend on luck, and I don't depend on my kids, but I definitely depend on doctors to get me through my recovery. They can only diagnose and give their opinions or advice. The rest is up to God and me. I don't know when my time on this earth is up. I know we all have a destiny, but it wasn't my time that day. That's why I work so hard. I hope I will successfully complete this journey, head up. I will have accomplished one of my life's most difficult challenges. It has truly been rewarding in so many ways, accessing the strength that I knew that I had within. I had to approach this with passion and a winning attitude. I feel that I was chosen in so many ways, since I have been dealing with this condition.

I am getting stronger daily. My mind is in a wonderful place. I am at peace. This has been an amazing ride, and my spirit has been in such a phenomenal place. Since the beginning of this journey, I have tried to inspire and I have been inspired by so many people. I have found strength through this experience, and I have learned what I am truly made of and what we all are capable of as human beings when we put our mind to it. My condition has encouraged me and enhanced my life considerably. I am truly at peace with where I am in my life, considering what I have come through physically and mentally. I see so much improvement in everything I do daily. I do not see myself as being disabled. I see myself as someone with a personal lifetime challenge. I will win. This is an opportunity of a lifetime.

I know that sounds crazy, but that is how I have always felt. This is such a challenge. The only way I can beat this is to stay motivated and not lose my cool. I have to keep a positive spirit. It is hard work, but this is life. I hope that this book will encourage all who read it through whatever they are dealing with in their life. I will not accept having a stroke as a death sentence. It has given me a new lease on life and a new perspective for life. I hope after reading this book and hearing what I came through, my story will strengthen you and give you more courage to overcome any devastating situation you might encounter. Inside all of us is something waiting to be released to motivate us if we want it. We have to believe in ourselves. I am getting my life back on track, and just meeting and talking to people on the streets gave me so much strength, confidence, and the courage to keep trucking.

At times, it seems as though I could hear that quiet voice within saying, "Lou, you are going to make it. You are going to be okay. You will relearn and rebuild your mind, your body, and your life. If you stay focused and use your energies in positive ways, you will regain your reading skills again and be able to hold a conversation. Just don't stop; everything pertaining to life as you once knew it, you can reclaim. You can reach different heights." My mind is redeveloping constantly. I am relearning how to process information that benefits me every day, and as I reflect on my life since the stroke, I know that I will always be a work in progress. There was an old saying from back in the day: "Be patient. God is not through with you yet." That still applies today. I will be patient and continue doing what I do and being thankful for what has been given back to me. I count my condition as a blessing. I do believe that I was chosen for this awesome journey, to bless others who are going through something in their lives. If you are ever knocked down and you are not knocked out, get up and at least make an honest effort. You might surprise yourself. Just don't give up without a fight. See if you can make it. I had to know for myself. I used to say that God chose me for this, so that I could help change the world through the passion and purpose He has placed within me to overcome this situation. My faith is the engine that drives me every day, and I keep in mind that my fears can be disabling if I let them, but failure is not a part of my character. This test has filled me with a burning passion deep inside, and I will never allow my passion to be watered down by my circumstances. I will remain focused and persistent, and I am being rewarded every day. Some days are a lot harder than others, so I have to work a little harder. I believe that whatsoever I desire when I work and pray I will be granted. I keep talking about attitude, work ethic, and the will in maintaining that winning spirit that has carried me to where I am today. I have truly been blessed. I am always disappointed when people react in such negative ways when they experience hardship in their life. They waste so much positive energy on "Why me?" but I say, "Why not you? This is life."

Many of us act as if we were born with the great expectation that life is going to be easy. Well, if someone told you that it was going to be smooth sailing, I've got a special announcement: that person lied! In this life, sooner or later, the messenger of misery could knock on your door. If he hasn't already, he is right around the corner. Keep living; you will get your visit soon. Know that it will come, and be prepared to handle it without personalizing it in the wrong way. That's just life. I believe that I am a positively charged person. I am capable of enduring even life's most difficult times or challenges. Sometimes, I may look like I am being held down for a while, but I am always standing up inside of myself. I may not be able to change the situation I am dealing with, but I am in control of the way I handle it. This stroke has been no joke, but I took it on with a positive attitude and good things are happening for me. I believe that the human spirit has the capacity to overcome and get us through almost anything that we are faced with if we put our minds to it.

I have proven that to be a fact. My spirit has elevated me in ways that sometimes even I can't explain. I am in control, and I don't mean that in a cocky, boastful way—or do I? God's grace has been sufficient in supplying my needs and keeping me focused, and I am eternally grateful. I know this condition will be a part of my life the rest of my life, but I can handle it. I was created to come through this situation, but I must admit it has been a little surprising how calm and focused I have been. I knew that I was strong, but the magnitude and level of my physical and mental strength has surprised even me a little. I am amazed at times how focused I have remained at the weakest time in my life. I was able to keep it all together with my strength and belief that God was working through me to inspire others all the time. I still believe that I was being used purposely, and I believe that one day, I am going to be able to understand everything I have been through more clearly for my own edification.

Sometimes, I just sit and wonder about what I have been allowed to come through and how focused I remained through the entire ordeal. I stayed in the faith zone, and that definitely made a difference as I progressed through the rocky roads of life. I discovered that we are well put together. I discovered who I really am as a man, and I continue regaining insight into myself that leads to self-mastery, expansion of my consciousness, and improvement in the quality and state of my awareness. I still have a long road ahead of me. I have committed myself to getting to understand a little more about how lupus affects the body, and I gain a little more knowledge about how research is on the brink of significant breakthroughs in the underlying science of the immune system. Public awareness and understanding and medicine can work together to control symptoms and increase knowledge of the effects of the disease. They have allowed better management of lupus over time. Today, people with lupus are leading healthier, longer lives than at any time in history, but we have to want our life to make a difference, so we have to know how to handle our life. Personally, since the stroke, although I have made lots of progress and have taken my recovery in stride, one day, I hope I will be able to play ball again, go fishing, and just do some silly things once again. Sometimes we take the little things for granted when it comes to life, but the little things seem to have the most significance, and as I reflect on my life during recovery, I can see that for quite a while, my subconscious was so far from knowing or perceiving and not aware. I was free from self-awareness for quite a while. I would say, "God, there's got to be more. This cannot be it for my life, and I was right. There is more, but it was not going to be just given to me. I had to work for it and perceive consciousness as more than just awareness. I see it as a potential energy force comprised of my thoughts, feelings, and impressions. I view consciousness as an active dimension of the human mind, not merely a passive vault where thoughts are stored. I had to reactivate my consciousness to become a driving force again so I could get my life back on track for my betterment and that of those around me. If one highly motivated mind can make a difference, consider how much more a collective force can accomplish. I want to live life instead of just being alive. I want my children to be proud of me. They have no idea how much of my strength they have been responsible for. They are my reason for living, not just being alive, and they will continue to motivate me every day, just because they are my life.

I wasn't just left on this earth for no purpose. You've got to be hungry. You've got to want to live. You have to know how to inspire yourself. I used to listen to tapes. For a long time, I didn't even understand what was going on, but anything that I thought was inspirational, I listened to anyway when I wasn't out walking. They gave me energy. They strengthened my will. They motivated me in every way. The hard times seemed so much easier when I listened to anything positive that talked about recovery because my life was being threatened. That helped me keep my focus and see what I was made of. It is in the rocky times or moments that you discover who you really are and what you have inside. When you gain insight into yourself, you will do what you have to do to stay alive. I believed that I could make it back from where I was. My vision strengthened me because it showed me where I was every day. I did not like what I saw. I did not lie around whining. I could see myself through my situation. I have never talked to anyone who has been faced with anything of any significance and has not had days, weeks, and even months when they had to plow through all kinds of oppositions. It just comes with the territory of life.

I am not a religious person, but I truly believe in God and His awesomeness. I believe we are tested at times, and sometimes, we have to change our entire approach to life. This could be my test, and I will never know if I just lie around complaining. Whatever we are faced with, we can't let our fear take total control. There are times we have to move on with caution but proceed. As time goes on, we have to proceed *boldly*. I was faced with that situation, and I just accepted the challenge of where I was and thought about how I was going to get through it. I took control of the situation. Fear did not have any special power over me unless I employed or empowered it by giving up. It was difficult, but not being able to take care of myself *now* would have been a disaster. I refuse to live my life on someone else's terms, so I took that positive step on life's freeway.

I stayed within the speed limit, but I was at the wheel. I will be independent again. This has been an amazing ride on life's highway, but it's not free. Trust me, I believe anyone can conquer fear if he or she wants to live. A stroke is fearful, but death is deadly. I knew I could beat it. I did it but not just to prove to you that I could do it. When I had the stroke and I came to understand what condition I was in, I had nothing else to lose. I had to prove it to myself. If I wanted to live, I had to see myself healed and on the other side of this illness every day. There is greatness within all of us. As we travel through life, sometimes we may not think so in the middle of the storm, but we are amazing specimens. Sometimes, we go through situations because that's just life. We have to know this and be willing to fight for our life. That's how we identify. I would not change anything that I have been through the last fifteen years or so of my life. It has made me stronger, and I appreciate life even more.

I had been reading this book off and on. It was given to me by a very good friend for my birthday a few years before I had the stroke: *The Amazing Laws of Cosmic Mind Power*. This book has given me energy. It has been the most amazing read while I have been on this journey. I can almost feel it strengthening me while I am reading. It has given me tremendous insight into what I must do to reclaim my focus. It is amazing how spoken words from others have also motivated me every day in a positive way. I have no regrets concerning what happened to me. I still have the ability to keep living on my own. I don't have a crystal ball to look into and see what the future holds for my life. I feel good now. My spirit is not broken. I feel strong in every way. It makes me wonder what the future holds for me. Sometimes, life is hard and full of fear at the same time. Believe me, you can get up, shake it off, and continue moving forward. I am learning how to get back in control of my life and how to interact with people daily, and that's really encouraging. It elevates my strength and energizes me. I maintained the right concept of myself. The greatest tyrant I could allow would be a false idea. I control my mind. I keep it from holding me hostage with the ideas that I hold about myself. I induce definite emotions within me, psychologically speaking. Emotions control my course along life's path for good or bad. If I was full of resentment, concerning my condition, I would not be here and definitely be not doing as well as I am.

I maintain control over my feelings and my mental attitude. Negative thoughts never stay with me for any length of time, pertaining to my condition. They used to for short periods, but even then, for some reason, it never affected what I knew I had to do if I wanted to regain my independence. This is a mind-over-matter journey, and I couldn't think about someone literally taking care of me. That wasn't going to happen. I take life a little more seriously than the day before, and things open up for me a little more each day. I could not sit around and depend totally on my doctors' diagnosis. If I did, I would not be where I am today. I had to renew my own options, concerning my condition, and I am glad I did. I get to see myself a little closer to total recovery every day. I believe when we are down, we can accomplish a lot more than we think we can if we change our attitude and trust God.

I've learned so much about myself while on this journey to my recovery. My attitude really would have affected my healing if my life situation had gotten the best of me. When you have suffered something as devastating as a stroke and your life is spared, that is the time to at least try to turn lemons into lemonade. A wrong attitude could have been a death sentence for me. It's hard to soar with the eagle with a bad attitude. You have to make a choice. Your attitude is key. It is your lifeline. A bad attitude and a bad situation do not mix. I chose life. I believe that I have something special inside of me. The stroke was the driving force behind my recovery, and I was determined to fulfill whatever I had to do.

Thinking of what I have come through the last seventeen years of my life, at times, I am in disbelief. I just stand and stare in the mirror at myself. It is still very hard to believe I am in the shape I am in today, but I never doubted my vision or myself in making this journey a reality. I hope I have encouraged others. I talked out loud to myself at times. I would say, "Lou, you will be okay. Look how far you have come in your condition. You will succeed if you want to. *Fear* and *failure* are only words. As long as you have God's grace, only you can prevent yourself from succeeding. Your faith is stronger than fear." But every so often, we all doubt ourselves. Take only a moment to regroup and move forward. Keep your eye on the prize, and you will make it.

I know my attitude and hard work kept me alive during the first few years after the stroke. There was always that risk of having another stroke, but I had to keep going and move from one after-stroke challenge to another. I had to be really careful about falling. Being on blood thinners, I could bleed to death. If my blood was too thin and I fell, I could acquire a blood clot and be unaware. It could grow to many feet throughout my body. Either way, too thin or too thick, it could cause me to have another stroke or kill me. I had to be really careful and take my blood thinners every day. Periodically, I would have my blood checked. I have been blessed. I can't express that enough. I know there is someone watching over me at all times, and I have to take my condition very seriously. Dealing with lupus is no joke. Whenever something is in my spirit concerning my condition, I see my doctor right away. He is more than my doctor. He has become my best friend. I am very thankful for him and his services.

CHAPTER 11

CONTINUING TO INSPIRE OTHERS

While Retaking Charge of My Life One Day at a Time

As I continue on this amazing journey, putting my life back together and getting back in control, I hope that I have been a beam of light for everyone I have come in contact with in my travels. They truly inspire me to keep the faith and keep on pushing. I have come a long way, and I hope as the mystery surrounding my life continues to unfold, the trails that I leave will never be erased from people's minds. I hope whoever reads this book for whatever reason will be even more aware of his or her inner strengths. This experience has truly made me a better man. It has been an adventure and an experience I will never forget. We never know what may change our life's path.

I could have had the mind-set where I complained bitterly about my ups and downs after experiencing a great loss of my health and my senses, but I found a way to maintain a positive, upbeat spirit on the way to—I hope—leading a totally balanced life once again in which serenity and tranquility will reign supreme in my life. I thank God for everything I have been through and the way I have handled this experience. I truly believe I was chosen to be an example for others, and I hope that I have been and can continue to be that beam of light that others can apply to their life. My condition has even encouraged me more than I could have ever hoped for. I wanted to live, not just barely exist. I wanted to live a normal life and create new energies that people can draw from. Every day, my thoughts generate feelings and my feelings affect my body's healing system in so many ways. It prepares me for newfound energies, for what I might experience this day. I remember reading somewhere that your brain can process information about five times faster than the speed of speech. After the stroke, I was really excited and determined to see if that was still available to me. Life after a stroke is no joke, and trying to get my thinking pattern back on track with my mind was not easy, but there was no quit in me. I have so much work ahead. I can do this, and I am at peace with myself. My memory is better or, maybe I should say it's getting better each day. I can hear better in my right ear. I can see much better out of my right eye, and my reading is getting better. I see improvement in everything that I do. I don't see myself as a disabled person. I see myself as a person with many challenges that I can overcome. I am inspired more and more each day and grateful for another opportunity on my life journey, and that alone strengthens my will to keep pushing forward. My accomplishments, mentally and physically, since the stroke have been incredible.

I try to express the best in myself each day, and I hope other stroke victims can learn something from me. I don't have to die because the doctor said so. This could be my ticket to an even better life. My situation inspires me so much. I am just finding the strength within myself daily to keep moving. I do not mind working a little harder each day at getting my life back on track. People always wish me the best when I am out walking, and that gives me even more courage and confidence to keep going. At times, I can hear that soft voice within my spirit. "You will be okay, Lou." I am not the same person I was before the stroke. I think that I am stronger and more comfortable with myself. I know that sounds crazy, but it's true. Don't ask me to explain because I can't, but I am getting to understand a little more about lupus, how it will affect my body and my life in the future, and what I can do to make my life better one day at a time. As I gain more knowledge and confidence about the disease, I am feeling better. I know that researchers are on the brink of significant breakthroughs in the underlying science of the immune system while public awareness and understanding of how medicine can work to control symptoms and increase knowledge of the effects of the disease have allowed better management of lupus over time. Today, people with lupus are leading healthier, longer lives than at any time in history, but we have to want to live. We can make a difference in other people's lives. Every day, there is something different and it's so hard, but it's such a blessing that I am still here and still have that winning attitude. I try to reach different heights each day pertaining to my recovery. It's a challenge, but I have been unwavering. I still have a long way to go. I have that hunger within to recover totally. The hunger is my motivating force. I don't need any one or anything to motivate me other than life and being independent. My motivation is absolutely compelling. I do not want the threat of anyone other than myself physically taking care of me. It is important that I empower myself to overcome the obstacles that I will encounter.

I do not want to go through the rest of my life wondering if I could have made it back to independent living if I had only tried a little harder. Life is not always fair, and it is unrealistic to think that it will ever be. Just give it your best when it comes to taking care of yourself. As I proceeded daily, I always believed that I was going to make it. As a winner, I never quit. A loser never gets started because he or she doesn't have a clue as to what is inside. A loser allows circumstances to shape his or her life or take his or her life and self-image. I was determined, no matter what it took and no matter how long it took or how hard I had to work. I was instinctively searching for a way to get back from the brink of death. Something inside of me was saying, "You must believe in yourself *right now, today.*" A temporary give-up can cost you your life. My consciousness was so far from knowing or perceiving, not aware, free from self-awareness for quite a while. *God, there's got to be more. This cannot be it for my life,* I thought, and I was right, but it wasn't just going to be given to me. I had to work for it. I perceive consciousness as more than just an awareness. I see it as a potential energy force comprised of my thoughts, feelings, and impressions. I view consciousness as an active dimension of the human mind, not merely a passive vault where thoughts are stored. I had to reactivate my consciousness to become a driving life force to get my life back on track for my betterment and to better help those around me. After all, based on what I have come through, if one highly motivated mind can make a difference, consider how much more a collective force can accomplish. I want to live life instead of just being alive. I want my children to be proud of me; they have no idea how much of my strength they have been responsible for, and they will continue being my strength day to day, every day.

I know that I can overcome this situation. I wasn't just left on this earth for no purpose or as a sideshow. I was left for people to see God's work unfold through me. I have been inspired so much by motivational speakers like Les Brown and Zig Ziglar. During my recovery, they gave me that extra push I needed. When I listened to them at times, I felt as though they were literally talking to me each time I listened, which was almost every day. Les was my favorite, but both of them lifted my spirit every time I heard them speak. I always think of a quote in Les Brown's book, *Live Your Dream*. It is during the rocky times when change comes into your life that you discover who you are. In the prosperous times, you build what is in your pocket. In the tough times, you strengthen what is in your heart, and that is when you gain insight into yourself, insight that leads to self-mastery and an expansion of your consciousness as a life force in both your personal and professional lives! Since the stroke, some days, I ask myself where I go from here and what I will do with what I have left. I want to do something with some of my music, and I would love to become a spokesperson for the Lupus Foundation or just a spokesperson for life after having come through such a devastating situation. I am not a stroke victim. I am someone who overcame becoming a stroke victim. I think I would make an exciting spokesperson. I bring passion and an amazing recovery truth, letting people know that their lives do not have to be over when something happens to you. You can have a productive life again. It could only be a test; make it an adventure. Sometimes we can be chosen for change and we can't recover for complaining. When you think that you have nothing left in the tank, you would be surprised how far the fumes will take you. I thank God every day for the fumes I had left and for recognizing that within myself that I can have a life after a stroke and being in a coma.

I truly believe this has been my blessing, my destiny in life, and I will use what I have left in that manner. I won't complain. I definitely have no regrets. I will never ever forget one step of this amazing journey. Courage is a powerful force if you apply it when you are in a devastating position. It isn't something that a man or woman loses, but sometimes, it can get misplaced when your will is being tested. Do not spend time looking at your problems or losses. Cease all negative thinking. Your mind cannot function harmoniously when it is tense. It relieves the strain to do something soothing and pleasant when you are presented with a problem. You do not fight a problem. You can overcome or use it to release pressure. Take a walk, if you are able, to keep your mind as alert as possible. I have to keep that in mind. I will always be faced with inabilities, but it's no pressure on me. I couldn't read and didn't understand when people addressed me, but I would keep busy even if what I did turned out wrong at times. An inner calm would take over, and I would become poised, peaceful, and confident. I have remained focused through my recovery. Even to this day, after all that I have been through, my future depends on how I handle my present condition. I choose to look forward not backward. I look with great expectancy to the future, and with wisdom and inspiration, as God guides me through this amazing journey, I know things will turn out in such a wonderful way. As God continues guiding me through my recovery, His presence in my spirit will keep me filled with joy. I am running over with confidence. I knew that God was with me in all phases of my recovery at all times. I could not have made it this far with a bad spirit and a negative attitude and remained so single-minded. I gave everything that I had daily to my recovery on this journey. If I had not, my condition could have quickly become a liability.

It is amazing how a positive, thankful attitude can improve everything that you touch in your life if you would listen intensely and stay focused. It takes a lot of courage, and it will take even more as I continue developing a constructive, creative outlet concerning my condition. This means doing anything that stimulates my brain's thinking ability. That helps me to concentrate and keep the right concept of myself while putting my life back together a few pieces at a time. During the past few years, I have lived with this condition. Periods of depression have tried to overwhelm me at times, but I seemed to always stay in control. I learned to deal with my blue moods more effectively daily from the beginning. I did not allow myself to be overwhelmed. I would not let it take me in its painful grasp. I became apathetic at times, immobile. I turned down invitations, avoiding contact with people I so desperately needed to be around, but I had to work through that for a while. I was too embarrassed for people to see me in my condition, especially people who knew me. This experience has truly taught me some amazing life lessons on how to deal with my situation, and I hope my story will encourage and let others know that in devastating situations, you can come back. You'll have no idea of your capabilities if you give up. You may be able to leave a trail for others to follow. That's just the way life is. I will always be eternally grateful for the opportunities and new experiences this stroke has generated. It has enhanced my life, and I hope I will continue in a positive way to keep encouraging people who are on a similar path. My attitude can be reformed every day based on my daily experiences.

As long as I live, I know I will be adopting changes or reinforcing my attitude daily, helping others. I have learned that there is no such thing as an unalterable attitude. I want to recover. The more I reinforce my mind with a positive attitude and good thoughts, the stronger I become in rebuilding my body and mind for new adventures on this awesome journey called life. I believe when we are faced with a situation in life that we think is bigger than we are, it just might be the test for the next phase of our life. That's how I used that thought in my recovery. My attitude and my thoughts have been readjusted so many times because of the changes to my body. Every day on the way back, at times, I felt my attitude was losing altitude, but I kept in touch with the tower. Pull up, and you'll be okay. My recovery depended on what happened in me, not to me. I believe what I sowed enabled me to reap positive benefits because I had sowed positive seeds during my recovery. I believe that was the difference between my success and my failure.

Things could have turned out so differently, but it has been so inspiring. It has been the determining factor for my life, not accepting failure as final. That was never an option for me. I can't separate myself from what happened to me, but I can approach my situation with a winning attitude and maybe earn another opportunity at life. I realize that my faith is stronger than my fear. That's the only thing that will guarantee me success through a somewhat doubtful undertaking. Deep down in my spirit, I knew I could beat this. I believe I was being tested. This is the miracle in my life. I can feel it. I felt good in my spirit. It was a feeling of confidence and love. God is greater than fear. My future is worth the fight. I had to be bold and give myself a chance to see how God would work in my favor if I just *believed*. I did, and He showed up.

Believe me; whatever you need to work with, you already have it. Trust yourself; you can overcome whatever you are faced with. You can. I will expect the best from myself daily. You will make it. Think positively. Be confident. Believe in yourself. Promote yourself. Just know that God is able, but only through you. Eliminate those negative words completely from your vocabulary when you are fighting for your life. *I can't. I will try. I don't think … I don't have the time. Maybe. I am afraid. I don't believe.* Learn to minimize *I* and *impossible.* Belief is inward conviction; faith is outward action. You will receive both encouragement and accountability, verbalizing your intentions when you are down. Anyone can fight the battle for just one day. It is only when you and I add the burdens of those two awful eternities, yesterday and tomorrow, that we tremble.

It is not the experiences of today that drive me to distraction. It is the remorse or bitterness for something that happened yesterday and the dread of what tomorrow might bring. Therefore, live but one day at a time—today— and continue hoping for tomorrow. There is a solution to every problem. This I know, decree, and believe. As I claim these truths boldly, I believe that I will continue receiving guidance pertinent to all my undertakings and wonders will continue to happen in my recovery, as long as I do not give up. It is very important how I see myself, especially my image as a man. That means everything to me. I did not rely on my family or my kids to take my disability as their own. After the stroke, I didn't depend on them at any time for my recovery or to help me. That's just the way I felt inside. I wanted to know what I could do for myself. Sometimes, when we are going through something, we look for too much help from others and lose our focus. We never get to know our own strength, and yes, we even look for too much from our doctors. The majority of the answer is within us, and that is why we fail ourselves. So much of the time, we need to trust our own instincts more instead of complaining. Test your inner strength. There is so much about ourselves that we just don't know. I said before that when you are already down, there's nowhere to go but up. Take the challenge. You just might succeed. I did. As a person thinks within him- or herself, so is he or she. This verse has had special significance for me during my recovery. Every day, I read something positive, the best that I could every day. I listened to positive people with a little understanding daily, trying to stay focused every day. It wasn't easy. I know that God has been with me on this journey; sometimes, I could hear voices in my spirit saying, "Don't quit." You have to want to get better. Your attitude toward life has to be positive. I know that the key factor in my recovery has been my attitude and my work ethic. That transformed into faith and willingness to do what I had to do to recover. It took strong resolve to be positive every day. I knew that my attitude would determine where I would end up. It was my choice, not my circumstances, that determined how I thought. Anyone can become a positive person if he or she wants to. God has helped my desire to stay strong to process what I have to go through, and as long as I stay faithful, I will make it. Sometimes, when people are in difficult situations, they have negative attitudes. They do not realize that attitudes know no barriers; the only barriers that bring our attitude into bondage are those we place upon them. Attitudes, like faith and hope, can cross over any obstacle. I realized this truth. Let me encourage you to take control of your attitude and begin the needed changes in your life. You can do it. You can tell when you are on the road to success.

It's uphill all the way. "It will take time to reach new heights. Be patient knowing that anything worthwhile is worth working for. Although change itself is not progress, it is the price we pay for progress." This is from a prayer by John C. Maxwell, "Up, Up, and Away." "Dear God, change is never easy yet growth demands it." Therefore, I fearfully stepped out of my world of defeatism and cautiously opened myself to a world of winners. It will take time,

Lord. Therefore, I will be patient, letting You and others help me restore my body, which is lacking in strength. I will need a lot of help; therefore, I will accept what You send me from heaven, a place of various things for my specific needs. Truthfully, Father, I'm still intimidated and lack strength. Therefore, I ask that You do something for me that I cannot do for myself. And as my attitude changes and a better me becomes a reality, I will give You all the praise. Amen. As Zig Ziglar says, "I will see you at the top."

CHAPTER 12

THYROID REMOVED

October 2013

I never knew the importance of the thyroid gland and the role it plays in our everyday life and body functions. At the same time, we can survive without it and have a normal, productive life, but I still felt uneasy about having it removed. I didn't know what to do after being diagnosed with an overactive thyroid gland. I have been having a problem since my early teen years. I never knew that the thyroid gland was my problem and wondered if the doctors really knew themselves at that time. This was the early eighties. I would lose ten or twenty pounds periodically in such a short time, and I didn't know why. I never really gave a second thought to why this was happening. I always stayed slim, so I didn't have any worries about being overweight. At the same time, I didn't know the seriousness of my situation. When I was diagnosed with lupus in August 1988, that caught me off guard, but that's life. I did a little more research on the thyroid gland, and everything that I had been experiencing for years or since my early thirties for sure was related to my thyroid gland not regulating my metabolic processes (organs) properly. Obviously, without a properly functioning thyroid gland, I was concerned, but I thought I was just tired from being so active. I didn't think that much about it after being diagnosed with lupus, which affected my kidneys. I thought that was my problem, period. But my situation was much more serious, and as I got older, I got more concerned and started educating myself on what could happen to me because of a malfunctioning or no thyroid gland. This can be quite displeasing. I was at that stage in my life. I was being treated, but that wasn't helping the situation. My doc recommended that I have my thyroid gland removed. I didn't know what to expect after studying the thyroid. I still didn't know how to approach this dilemma. When I had the stroke, no one thought that I would make it but me, so I decided I would approach this with a positive attitude. When my thyroid was removed, minutes after waking up in recovery, I knew something had drastically changed in my body. I felt so different after the surgery. My energy level got a huge boost. I felt like my entire body had been overhauled. I felt amazing immediately. My personality changed. I know this sounds exaggerated, but my attitude changed. All my body functions changed. I felt like a new man. I never thought I would feel this good ever again, so am I going to worry about my thyroid being removed? No, I will live my life to the fullest of my ability day to day, on my terms. This is what it is. I have confidence in the creator and myself. I know my situation is really serious, but if I still had my thyroid gland, life would still be over when it was over. There is no guarantee with or without it. I feel good today. To me, that's all that matters. I will do everything I can to maintain a healthy lifestyle, exercising and helping myself to stay in as good of shape as I possibly can. The purpose of life is to live a life of purpose as best we can, but things will still happen. I believe that whatever we go through in life there is a reason for. I am not referring to absolute foolishness on our part, but life itself at times may deal us a hand we feel we don't deserve. Play it. You can win. You have to endure patiently. Let us run. If you can't run, do whatever you can do with patience with the situation that's before you, and I guarantee you that success will follow. I believe that God is looking for someone whom He can use to transfer His passion through, people to whom He can give a vision and a dream to be fulfilled and carried out. Life is a gift, and sometimes we may be called to give.

On June 24, 2000, while still recovering from a stroke, I lost my twin brother, Lewis. Already weakened from the stroke mentally and physically, I felt a part of me was gone and thought I wouldn't make it because I did not feel complete without him. Dealing with the stroke and the death of my brother was more than I thought I was capable of handling at that time. So much of my strength and will was hard to regain until I thought of our last conversation. He assured me he was all right.

My twin brother Lewis Moore died
June 24, 2000, I miss you so much

poetic images photography

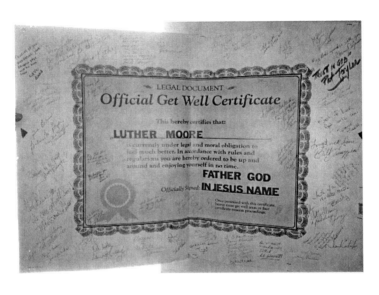

Get well card from co-worker after
coming home from hospital.
THANKS! TO ALL P.H.A STAFF FOR YOUR
KINDNESS, DURING MY ILLNESS.

CHAPTER 13

WHERE DO I GO FROM HERE?

Being diagnosed with lupus and suffering from a stroke have given me a rare form of personal security in maintaining my ability and relying entirely upon myself to meet my own needs. Self-reliance has undoubtedly been one of the most important ingredients in my life since being labeled disabled. Self-reliance is its own reward.

The physical burden of the lupus and the stroke and their grave seriousness have changed my life. Suffering such devastating setbacks, I am left with myself. I have time for self-identity and periods of total aloneness. It has had a way of forcing me into myself. This has been an invigorating experience, an opportunity. I feel like I was reborn as a different person, thinking new thoughts. New insights have emerged and given me a stronger sense of self. I have been presented with a multitude of exciting choices if I want to live independently again. Knowing that I have complete control over the way I choose to go forward has given me a sense of power.

I have the privilege of redesigning my own way or lifestyle on the basis of who I am. I can choose my opportunities and relationships and how they will be rather than have either forced upon me. I want the opportunity to enhance and govern that portion of my life that I have left. Since I have known real independence before, it is hard to relinquish that without a fight and definitely without ever trying. I know that it will be impossible to regain everything I lost, but my life, my physical being, is literally predicated on how I handle myself day by day, in living as normal a life as I possibly can. This is a lifetime disease that requires patience and being truly obligated to the cause.

Clearly, this condition is quite an educational experience. I have to stay out of the sun as much as possible when it exceeds certain temperatures. I am learning more and more about how not to allow the seriousness of these diseases to overwhelm me. This has become a way of life for me, and it is important for me to stay focused, identifying flares when they begin. That is part of the burden of lupus and recovering from a stroke simultaneously. It has become a life experience, but I don't worry about it. I know that I will always experience certain symptoms because of these diseases for the rest of my life. Because of their complexity, it is not clear what to do at times. Other than being extra careful of the hot sun and sodium intake, I find that working out as much as possible really helps me tremendously. Exercising my muscles every day has been key to helping me to move on with my life.

This has been a hell of an experience, but I take it day by day and I am okay with that. It only strengthens my will even more and helps me to stay focused. The journey has been an eye-opener for me. Learning how the subconscious mind works is absolutely amazing. I started understanding how to use it to my advantage. The subconscious is actually 90 percent of the mind. That leaves just 10 percent for the conscious mind to operate in making my daily decisions. The brain is the most important part of my anatomy. It tells all the other parts what to do and when to do it. The brain works as part of a network that includes the spinal cord and peripheral nerves, which I had trouble with for a while. They transmit and control any information sent to and from the other areas of the body. Nonetheless, the brain is the master controller and my guide.

I am learning through repetition more and more how it works through me to help with my healing process and dealing with both conditions simultaneously. I have to do things over and over frequently at times until I get them right. Regardless of how long it takes, eventually things come together. I would get control of another little piece of what I had lost. I am getting to understand more and more of what is required of me each day if I care to remain independent. The task at times is overwhelming, but I keep moving. I am always on automatic. I repeat positive affirmations and statements to myself regularly to reinforce the positive beliefs in my mind. I am spiritually guided daily. I know that everything that I have accomplished has been because of God's grace and the subconscious mind.

It always kept me in reach of things even if I couldn't always reach them consciously, but I kept trying until finally everything became a reality. We won't understand it until such times as the one I was faced with, but there was something in my spirit that kept reminding me to listen to learn. Learn to listen, and you will make it. It is absolutely amazing what I have accomplished in the condition I was in. I am living proof you can lose almost everything and come back if you don't lose sight of God and maintain a positive attitude. I still believe I was chosen for this journey.

I have said this so many times I can never overstate that too much. For me, I believe the best is yet to come. There is so much God-given talent inside all of us that does not get released until we prove we are deserving. I never really understood how that worked until my life was threatened. I was weakened and strengthened at the same time. I never lost sight of God's grace. He had already given me more than I needed to overcome this situation.

We are more capable than we think when we are in the most difficult times of our journey through life. If it's not your time, you are not going anywhere. Just have the desire and the will that has already been awarded to you. Stay single-minded, and recognize that one power, and then your mind will move as a unity with God. I did not spend time looking at my situation as a problem. I used it as an opportunity. I believe that the reason a lot of people do not make it is because they do not believe in themselves. They put everything on God and don't realize that we are the vehicle He works through. If we don't show any effort, he has nothing to work through. That's just the way it is, and I know this from experience. We burn up most of our positive energy sitting idle and complaining. Without the right mind-set, we cannot function harmoniously. When we are giving no effort to our own healing, how can we expect God to work for us if we idle when we are faced with difficult situations? I believe God created us with such unique abilities, but sometimes we don't focus so we cannot see the bigger picture. All we can think is *Why me?* instead of *Why not me?* We don't give ourselves a chance to see God's powers unfold in our lives. We can handle a lot more than we think. When I had the stroke, it gave me a tremendous opportunity to reestablish true personal independence again and learn to take care of my own needs and to assume total responsibility for myself without looking to others.

I am in a position to acquire the sort of inner strength that results from being my own source of support, regaining true independence again to achieve a sense of being complete and whole within myself. It won't come easily or overnight. Believe me; it comes as a result of years of thoughtful, responsible, solitary living in order to become independent once again. I had to rebuild a solid confidence in myself once again, learning to do things on my own and how to share my life with another. I will remind myself of what I want to accomplish every day and work toward it instead of waiting on God to step in when He has already supplied me with all I need to empower myself. I won't accomplish it by complaining.

I know that the energy and power of God permeates every atom, tissue, muscle, and bone of my being and can heal me through my faith, my belief, and my works in a positive way. I can't just wait to be healed; it does not work that way. Sometimes the situations that we are faced with are on us. I don't believe that God will put more on us than we can handle, but He never gets the chance to really see His powers at work in some of us, because all we do is complain. I believe I was chosen for this journey. Even if I wasn't, I would still be afraid to quit because it is the only way I will know my own essential strengths and the infinite riches within myself. We tend to magnify the problems instead of magnifying God's gifts and powers within us.

In the difficult times that confront us in life, imparting to the problem more power over us, we fail to contribute to our own healing. Our thoughts and feelings create our destiny. There is no one to blame but ourselves. I believe that we create our own heaven or hell by the way we think and the things we do or do not do. Retribution or reward, it depends on how we use our minds. The law of action and reaction is universal throughout nature. Think good, and good will follow. Think bad or negative, and I believe that follows also. The feeling of security or insecurity is due primarily to our basic approach to everyday life. It is amazing how the thankful attitude is improving my healing every day during my recovery. Believe me, whatever you are dealing with, approach it every day head-on with authority and a positive attitude and you won't lose.

You must believe in yourself and not the fear of failing. You are already down, so what do you have to lose by trying to rise up? Believe in the magic that's within, and you will discover what you are truly made of. Don't be afraid to reach your full potential in life. You have to find a lasting basis on which to build your self-worth. Just as my belief has moved me forward on my journey, your belief can hold you back or move you forward. Don't let the fear of failure rob you of the possibility of succeeding. You have to be totally involved in your own healing. I challenge you to test your will when you think you have nothing left. You can decide your future no matter how hard it may seem. If you are still alive, take control. I tell myself every day that this is only a test. It's a piece of cake. I feel good about where I am today, but I still have a long ways to go. No one thought that I would make it, and if I did, I would not be able to live on my own.

I can deal with my condition and what I have to work with. I am okay. It is very important that I keep in mind where I am physically and mentally. Sometimes, devastation can end up being the most inspirational time of your life. I am grateful that I am still alive and have a wonderful attitude every day. I know life's journey is not just some long, trouble-free, insignificant trip that we are on. We are connected to a long line of unforeseeable experiences that may happen and that we will feel we didn't deserve, but that's life. When you are in the midst of the storm that may be your blessing, you can make it. That may be your test. Ask yourself, "What am I going to do with what I have left?"

We are not on this earth just to take up space or just to use up oxygen. We all should want to be a difference-maker and strive to encourage others. I didn't know from one second to the next when my life would end, but if there is anything positive that I have left from my situation, I will make it. If God says yes, I will truly prepare myself mentally to make a difference in others' lives. If I never learn anything else in life, I have found out what I was capable of in my darkest hours. I didn't want to look back on my life wondering if I could have made it and helped someone else discover what's inside of him or her. It begins with a burning desire and willingness to live. I did not let any thought undermine my desire or abilities to pass this test. I truly believe that I was chosen for this challenge and I can do this if I want it badly enough. If there was one quality, one distinguishing characteristic, one accomplishment in my life that can excite God more than any other, I believe that it has been the way I have handled my condition. It awakened things in me I didn't even know were in me, but whatever it was infused my life with power and purpose, unrelenting, undying drive and passion. I have come though things mentally and physically that no one thought that I could overcome, but as a man thinks within himself, so he is. The thoughts that consistently controlled my mind were always positive. *I can do this.* I knew that I was capable of accomplishing what was at hand. I knew that I had to be passionate if I wanted to ignite the release of God's explosive powers within me.

I believe as God sees passion in our efforts, he rewards us. I believe that's why I have done so well in my recovery. It's available to all of us based on our actions, our efforts, and our willingness to live life to the fullest again in the midst of devastating odds. Keep in mind that *faith is your mind.* God can't see our motives if we don't try; He can't see our feelings, faith, confidence, aspirations, longings, or the life principle within us when things happen in our lives. Everything that I have overcome has been because of my faith, my belief in myself, and my willingness to win. I have heard a lot of people concerning their situation say, "God will take care of me," but faith without works is dead. When you are down, you have to make an effort any way you can with whatever you have left. I believe God will renew your strength.

My self-esteem made me successful on this journey, and the way I interpret my condition seems to strengthen me more each day. The subconscious mind works to control my life. All the habits and beliefs I held in my subconscious mind suddenly were released, and I took control. I am where I am, regaining my true independence, and it has not been easy to achieve. A sense of being complete and whole within oneself doesn't come overnight. It comes as a result of years of thoughtful, responsible solitary living. Becoming independent also required that I build a solid confidence within myself, relearning to do things once again on my own. Living alone again can breed a type of independence that takes root in my sense of self-confidence and grows with my freedom to do as I wish with my life. Once you've known real independence, you will not want to relinquish it if there is even a slight possibility of overcoming your illness. Being self-reliant is its own reward.

There is nothing like knowing for a fact that you can take care of yourself, depending on your own resources for your personal security. In no longer looking to others for what can only come from you, you discover your abilities to be an enormous source of comfort and satisfaction. To be able to say to yourself, "I am a resource of mine; I can depend on me" is most gratifying and tends to be an enhancement to feelings of security and self-esteem. During my recovery, I discovered that no other person can give me the security that I could provide myself, and I gained incredible personal strength within my spirit, choosing to live alone. Many people live their entire lifetimes never knowing the peace that comes with private moments with oneself.

If I had been living with someone during my recovery, I don't believe I would be doing as well as I am today. It was hard times, and it was a great time. I learned so much about myself and my strength. This experience has been the most amazing time of my life. This added a new chapter or dimension to my life that required amazing courage. When the absolute essence of my existence was being threatened daily, I found ways within to conceive and believe it could be achieved. It will deliver, and that is a literal truth. The power of the subconscious mind enabled me to develop a deeper appreciation and understanding of what life really is and what I had left inside of me. If I wanted to be independent again, it was all up to me understanding the power of the subconscious mind and how it works. That was the beginning of my recovery, and I mean that literally, getting a clear understanding of what was required of me in the scientific rim of my mind as the feminine or right brain aspect of the mind, which could be considered as the translator or middleman for the conscious mind. It is often referred to as God, universal consciousness, or whatever the source of my understanding might be. As I progress in my recovery, I learn that the brain and the mind are not the same. The mind is spiritual in nature. I have learned that the power of the subconscious mind can work either way for me. The subconscious mind does not know the difference between what I perceive as good or bad, right or wrong, and so on. It is created to store exactly what I give it, and that is exactly what it does. That is why, as I learn more and more how it operates for me through me, I keep my mind loaded with things pertaining to my recovery. I can see what I want to accomplish.

When I came home from the hospital and rehab, the conscious part of my brain started allowing me to make decisions, but I did not know how to implement them for a long time. Until my subconscious mind took over, my eyes, ears, and sense of touch and taste were not perceiving anything. I had to fight to transmit signals to my brain. It's my subconscious brain that actually turns those signals into picture, sensations, or auditory experiences that could be understood and become useful to me in my recovery. The brain is the most important part of our anatomy. It tells all the other parts what to do and when to do it. The brain works as part of a network that includes the spinal cord and peripheral nerves. Together, they transmit and control any information sent to and from the other areas of the body. Nonetheless, the brain is the master controller of our lives.

There are all sorts of conditions we may experience in life, and to get through a stroke, I had to get involved with them all in occupational therapy, speech therapy, and physical therapy. I was involved in all simultaneously for quite a while. It was no joke. There are many different factors that affected my recovery, but I had to keep my focus. My attitude was key. Every day, my main factor was the severity of the stroke and what damage occurred to my brain obviously. The more serious the stroke, the more damage that is done and the lower the chances of recovery. I was told this by my doctor. My rehab recovery to some extent was in my hands. Trained professionals could help me, but about 90 percent of my recovery was my hands and depended on my will to recover.

I had to want to recover badly. It was on me. It was and still is hard, but determination and perseverance are the key factors for me. I was left here for a reason. It was very demoralizing and embarrassing for a long time to let people see me in the shape I was in, but to recover, I knew that I had to maintain a positive frame of mind. That too was exhausting but productive. I was determined not to lose my life or my independence if I was given another chance at life. It wasn't going to be easy. I would lose what positive energy I had left by lying around and sobbing. My mental and physical strength would have deteriorated, and I would have never known if I could have made it or not because I would have died. The fear of inadequacy is a common trap for some stroke victims, like myself. It almost trapped me. I felt guilty and useless for a long time after the stroke, and I did not want people to see me in the shape I was in. I could hardly walk because I had no balance. My speech was slurred and imparted badly. My memory was gone, but I was left with enough to know that I wanted to live. It took years for me to really feel comfortable with my condition, but I kept working and pressing forward, keeping my mind as clear as possible. My life was a fog, but I kelp a good attitude. I had to if I wanted to be independent again.

During my recovery, I am learning that there is more to life than we can see with our natural eyes or ever know with our finite minds. My life will be a constant challenge and reminder of how blessed I have been on this journey. It so hard, but it is not hard enough for me to give up. This has been the most inspiring time of my life. Half the time, I didn't even know what I was doing, but I stayed positive and in control as much as I could. This is my life. What other alternative do I have, other than keeping the right attitude and the right spirit? It has been unreal, and I have been unwavering. I talk openly about my condition and having been in a coma from the stroke, even though it is difficult to deal with. Not talking about it makes it even more complex. Talking about my condition has been a major part of my healing. Trying to separate that from my life is impossible. Talking about it makes my life a lot easier and has inspired others.

When I talk to people about my journey, I try to leave them with a feeling that if they are ever faced with a situation like I was, they could make it also. I would have never known if I hadn't tried. It's up to me to use my subconscious mind power. Remember that it reasons deductively. It sees the end results only, thereby bringing to a logical, sequential conclusion the nature of the premise in the conscious mind. I started to understand the part of my brain that was affected and the size of the injury. Learning the location of the injury to my brain gave the medical team information about skills that I would likely be unable to accomplish. My age was a big factor to my recovery. After talking to the doctors, I started to understand a little. They did not think that I would recover enough to be independent again and definitely not enough to live on my own or drive again. I had trouble speaking and was constantly confused. I could not understand. I could not judge distance. I had trouble walking. I suffered from dizziness and had no coordination on the right side of my body. There was no feeling, and I could not use my hand. I could not hear, and walking and talking at the same time was difficult. A lot of my recovery was up to me. I ignored a lot of my instructions when I was told by doctors not to try certain things. My spirit was telling me the opposite, that I could come back if I wanted to. As I started really recovering, I learned that wisdom is avoiding all thoughts that weaken me. There are certain conversations I don't have with certain people. You must be mindful. I needed encouragement more than ever or anything. I wanted to live life on my terms, not just exist in life.

I wanted to regain my independence in such a way that fear could not dominate me. There are many primitive fears in the subconscious mind of all of us. When things happen to us of this magnitude, we can eradicate all those fears by knowing that mentally and emotionally, God's presence is always within us and so clear. I was given the ability to know this without a doubt. I just trusted my spirit implicitly, and I knew I would make it. Within my spirit, I knew I had to earn it. I was free and fearless. I didn't even have a clue in so much of my recovery what I was doing, but I believe it was a test to see if I would quit. Today, I know where I am going. I know where I came from. The mind is a terrible thing to waste, which we do by complaining and not even making an effort. The seriousness of my situation in my mind was only a test. I may sound crazy, but that's how I feel. I showed so much courage all through my recovery. To this day, I still don't understand how I did the majority of the things I was able to do.

My mind was not that clear, but what I would attempt seemed to always end up right. My reaction or my response was wise. My action was only the outer expression of my thoughts, and my constructive actions and decisions were only a gift from God. They were a manifestation of a wise or true thought, entertained in my mind after I had asked for guidance through this awesome challenge, knowing that would activate my subconscious. It knew what I wanted to accomplish and had the know-how the moment I came to that definite conclusion in my conscious mind. I knew that I could be independent again. When my subconscious mind took control, the power and wisdom that I needed to continue was granted.

For the rest of my life, I must maintain a winning spirit, staying calm and comfortable with my condition, accepting where I am in my life. Since the stroke, I have remained mentally focused. I write down my collective thoughts when certain substantive thoughts enter my mind that I really don't want to forget. I watch my stress levels to keep a good balance in my life. I don't look at what happened to me in a negative way. If I did, I would not be where I am today in my recovery. I really feel good, and that's all that matters to me. I do not have negative talks with myself or with anyone else concerning my condition. I always visualize what I have been allowed to accomplish since I have been on this journey.

Taking care of myself physically, emotionally, mentally, and spiritually every day, at times, has been very draining, but it has been the best time of my life. Deep inside, I know how blessed I am, being in my condition. This is my life, and I know that only by God's grace am I winning the fight one day at a time. I am maintaining my ability to think and see things more clearly each day. When I really think on where I am today, it's hard to get it. I had no idea what was inside of me, but if I didn't reach for it or believe that I could do it, I would have been dead. Nothing comes easily in life. When your life is being threatened, everything from then on seems as though you are trying to move a mountain. That is not the time to lose your courage or complain. That only puts more pressure on you. It only weakens you further; you can make it. My sexual life was gone. I didn't even know how to approach it. It is no joke trying to regain or recover from such devastation. I am getting it back together, slowly but surely. It has been a hell of an experience for me, but I believed that I could overcome it and regain my life so I could live with dignity. God has given me tenacity. I still have a purpose, and I still believe that I was kept for a reason. I am to be a light for others. I don't know why I feel this way, but it has been such a blessing for me. Maybe I was allowed to recover for others to see He is still in the blessing business. When I realized that God had kept me, I knew he wanted me to be an example for others in my life. When we are at our lowest point in our lives, His powers coming through us are not hard to explain.

As long as I am alive, I will always keep in mind that no matter how hard things get, I can't quit. I have to retrain my brain every day. It can be the same with you. Sometimes, we misread the message of our circumstances and miss a golden opportunity because the task at hand is not easy. You are already equipped with whatever you need to recover when things get tough in your life. Our subconscious mind is our life. Be careful of the reason you give up on yourself. I believe when we give up on ourselves, we also limit God's ability to work in our lives. I am learning that on the road to my recovery in my life. I think about how much I believe that God left me here for a reason. I am afraid of not doing the right thing. I am waiting on God. Previously, I told you that you already have what you need to overcome your situation. I truly believe that with everything in me, I can stop complaining. Faith is my mind, and I do not have to become a victim to my circumstances or my condition.

Faith is a healer with work and the right attitude. It must work through me if I want to get better. It is a manifestation of my faith in the unseen or unknown. I believe that this omnipotent presence called God is responsive to my thoughts and my healing if I work and believe that I will be okay. I am learning through this experience every day that my faith is an attitude of my mind that commands results and gets them only if I want it. I do not need more faith.

I have plenty, but I must use it constructively and give it purposeful direction. I feel and believe that my God-self illuminates my pathway. Divine intelligence inspires, directs, and governs me in all my undertakings. It instantaneously reveals to me the answer to all the things I need to know, pertaining to my healing. Divine love has always gone ahead of me, making sure all roads are a highway of peace.

My recovery has been hard and so wonderful at the same time. I believe and accept without question that there is a creative intelligence in my subconscious mind, which knows all and sees all. I know that I am being directed rightly to my true place in life, and I accept this inner guidance without question. I was left here for a purpose, and I am fulfilling that purpose. My mind is in a very peaceful place at all times, and I give thanks for being allowed to know that I can recover from such a devastating situation and be at peace with whatever I am released with pertaining to my health. I have such a good spirit. This is representative of the miracle of divine guidance, which is available to us all in devastating times if we listen. I believe that when things happen in life, if we devote ourselves and do not complain, we can make it through much more than we think. Your subconscious mind answers you in ways you know not of. You may be led many places to get things that will help you in your recovery. Some might seem ridiculous. You may overhear a conversation that provides you with information to help you recover. Things may come in countless ways. It is necessary to stay alert. Once I got to understand that, I began discovering a new hope. It was amazing.

I learned that in life, some circumstances are beyond my control, but I have to stay in control of what I can. I refused to believe that the doctor's diagnosis had to be my death sentence. I believed that hope was my choice, and I choose hope not hopelessness. My aim is to have a mind fully submitted to that recovering spirit within me, not just to see better lab results or improvements based on what the doctor says. I wanted to see and feel it in my spirit every day, and that was up to me. I believe that I was put on this earth to come through what I am dealing with, but it is up to me how I handle it. When your mind is full of hope, it will protect you and fight your sicknesses. God's word says that hope produced in the midst of suffering does not disappoint us; it bears fruit. I believe that. Common sense tells me that the person whose heart is fixed upon hope will produce more positive healing and positive emotions on the journey to recovery. It's up to me. I want other patients to know that having lupus and then a stroke does not mean you cannot live a normal life, despite all the changes.

I still have hope. I have been through a lot since I was diagnosed with lupus and had the stroke. I used to fight with myself until I learned how to handle my situation. I do not intend to let it control me. Should any of you ever be diagnosed with lupus, the most important thing is not to despair. Helpful medications are available, and a positive attitude really helps. I try to smile even on my down days. I keep smiling at life. Keeping the faith has kept me strong, even during lupus flares.

Depression can sabotage my recovery and make the lupus symptoms worse. Every day, I try my best to live as normally as possible, being positive and courageous and maintaining a good relationship with my doctor. I keep being kind to myself. I shall succeed and be happy. I remember the most important thing; I put my trust in just one God. It has been over seventeen years since I had the stroke and about thirty-five years since I was diagnosed with lupus. I think that I am doing great. It's all about attitude. If you live again, it's up to you. How do I cope with the depression that might kick in every now and then? I stay in control of my situation mentally, emotionally, and physically. It is not easy, but it is easier than sitting at home complaining. This journey really has been an amazing adventure and will continue to be. I believe that one day, research will find a cure for this disease, but until then, I will continue doing what I have to do to maintain a positive attitude every day. I am learning more and more through my healing that universal mind power is the greatest power in the world. Whatever you desire, your mind power can fulfill that need for you if you stay focused.

It will show you how to think, what to think about, and how to direct your energy so that you can deal with what is happening in your life and still maintain your dignity. I found priceless knowledge in the pages of my mind. It helps me banish fear and worries, which were deadly mental poisons to my recovery. I stay focused at all costs in my mind. That gave me physical strength and showed me how to use it effectively on this journey. It has paid me fabulous dividends pertaining to my recovery. It has proven very hard, but it has been an amazing ride for me every day, moving me forward with joy and enthusiasm. As I continue on this journey and with the writing of these words, my mind is purposefully in the most peaceful place I have ever been in my life.

I am learning so much about faith, *true faith*, the subconscious, and how they work together. True faith is based on the knowledge of the way my conscious and subconscious mind function and on the combined harmonious functioning of these two levels of the mind scientifically directed. It is the subconscious mind that does the healing, combined with eating healthy, well-balanced, and nutritious meals. Exercising regularly is the key to regaining my physical and mental strength. Whatever you believe is operating instantly in your subconscious mind. You can demand action. I want healing now. Hurry up. Thank you. I truly believe that we can demand certain things and receive them. The healing power of God is written all over us if we remove any mental blocks and let the healing power flow through us. We must believe that that is the only way it can work. The power of your subconscious is your life, and it goes where your vision directs it. I know in my heart that the God power flows through the patterns of thoughts and imagery in my mind, and I am under a divine compulsion to succeed.

I form the picture in my mind every day of what I want to achieve. The power of the subconscious mind is well aware of what it can accomplish through me because it is me. Do you know what you can accomplish if you listen? I don't let the word *incurable* frighten me. I realize that I am dealing with the creative intelligence that made my body. Although some people will say that a healing is impossible, be assured that this infinite healing presence is instantly available. I can always draw on its power through the creative law of my own mind, and I make use of this power now. It has performed miracles in my life. Miracles cannot prove that which is impossible. It is a confirmation of that which is possible; with God, all things are possible. We are all natural-born healers for the simple reason that the healing presence of God is within all of us, and all of us can contact it with our thoughts.

It responds to all of us. This healing presence is even in animals and plants. It is omnipresent and is the life of all things. It takes different degrees of faith. I learned through my recovery that it is easy for the healing presence of God to heal. There is no great or small in the God that made us all; there is no big or little, no hard or easy. Omnipotence is within all of us, but we have to want it. We have to move. It works because we are special. It works through us. I can speak on this from my own experience. It is the subconscious mind that does the healing with work through your belief. There are no incurable diseases. There are incurable people who believe they can't be healed, and according to their beliefs, it is done unto them. What they look for, they find. Your faith can move mountains, literally, through you. When I first had the stroke, once I got to know how the subconscious works, I had to use my intellect to carry out the voice of intuition and stay focused. The wisdom of my subconscious rose to the surface mind or consciousness, when the latter was relaxed and at peace. I could literally feel myself elevating.

When my thoughts were wise, my reactions or responses were wise. My action was only the outer expression of my inner thoughts. When things happen in your life, a changed attitude changes everything. Become enthusiastic. Believe in yourself and in your hidden abilities and powers. Wonders will happen in your life. You must learn about your own essential greatness and the infinite gifts within you. I never affirmed inwardly anything that I did not want to overcome outwardly. My lips and my heart agreed on a harmonious solution, and I got busy. I believe that life is always eminently fair, even the ups and downs and the sickness, turmoil, and misfortune. Just don't give up. I am concerned about my health and having a serious disease.

It became important for me to take an inventory of my innermost beliefs. Just before I examine those commonly held negative beliefs, I establish some guidelines within myself. Every day, I ask myself, "Is this illness bigger than God?" and the answer is no. My condition was deadly, but I believed I could overcome this condition. I refused to believe this was a death sentence. I believe God is on the side of my healing and as long as He is on my side, I will make it. I believe my hormones and immune system are on the side of my healing and are even working to help me handle this illness as long as I remain responsible for my treatments and manage them. I believe hope is a choice, and I choose hope, not hopelessness.

My beliefs create my thoughts, my thoughts generate feelings, and my feelings affect my body's healing systems. What I believe and tell myself can become a powerful tool in my healing. I know I can physically recover from this enough to live an independent life. Maybe I will always have the disease, but it will not have me. Mentally, I can handle the condition gracefully. I can live an independent, productive life. This is not a death sentence unless I choose to let it be. It's my choice. I believe I am on this earth to share my hope and joy with others through my recovery, and I always project positive energy because of my condition. It's the attitude. I believe that God's will is good.

I believe that He loves me and wants me to recover fully to live a rich, productive life of service and to inspire others. Whether I recover totally or not, I am going to live life with dignity and be as productive as possible each day. For as long as I am given another day on this earth, there is so much healing power in a healthy mind even when your body is being attacked. This is only a test. We have a God who cares about us. It would be wise to take a look at what He says about the connection between a healthy spirit and a healthy body—and about the human spirit in general. Over the past ten to fifteen years, I have learned so much about the amazing effect of the mind on the body. I read somewhere that two truths that have emerged from the scientific study of these issues by investigators are that most diseases do not result from a single causal factor. Even so-called terminal illnesses are not in themselves sufficient to cause death. There are other factors in maintaining or regaining your health, but the mind has an important influence on improving your physical health, an influence that we often neglect. Most of us go through life without giving a thought to the secret weapon God has planted inside us. It is built into every one of us. There is equipment that is designed to give us incredible protection and strength from or to handle diseases, and I believe this equipment, which is our immune system, works better if we deliberately give it more attention. You and I can help ourselves much more by making better use of our preinstalled equipment! I want to help you understand how your body's protective system works. I am only speaking based on my experience and what I have been through and am still going through. With such positive results, there is little room left to doubt that the immune system is under the direct control of the brain. Based on my thoughts and what I wanted to accomplish during my recovery, my mind remained connected to positive thoughts. The results have been amazing. Your mind can also render your natural bodyguards unable to do the work they are capable of or designed to do. I believe that a lot depends on our attitude and our will to recover. It would be too much to insist that the mind can cure every disease nevertheless.

We can overcome much more than we think we can through ourselves. To sum it all up, among other causal factors, our health is controlled by our brains. Let me add that our brains are controlled by our minds and spirits. Now let's look at the ways in which faith empowers our spirits. Yes, I believe that *Jesus* really died on the cross. Yes, I believe the Bible is God's word. That is doctrinal belief. The other aspect of faith is using what I know to be true—relying on God, trusting in Him. I tell myself every day that God left me here for a reason and I must do my part. Every day, I tell myself that what happened to me I can't blame God for. I wait for Him to show me the good this can bring, whether my condition totally vanishes or not. So far, I have been truly blessed dealing with this condition. Ninety-nine percent is about the attitude. When I got to really understand what had happened to me, I always had a special feeling in my spirit that I could and would make it back and live a productive, independent life. I had to make myself start taking risks. I had to get busy living or die, not even understanding at the time. I had to trust God to see me through. Had I not taken the risks and made decisions I was afraid to make, I believe I would not be alive today. I would tell myself every day, "You can do this." Life is not worth living depending on someone else for your every move. In my spirit, I believe life is in part mine for the choosing. As I get better, I tell myself God want me to have a good life and prosper, but that can't happen if I lie around and complain. I treat every single day of my life as a gift so precious because it is and has truly been for me. Since the stroke, sometimes, I believe life can contradict the doctors' diagnosis and absurdities through your faith. If I don't give up, maybe God won't give up on me, not quite yet. According to His will, as I understand it, I hear Him saying, "Go for it, Luther! Your faith is your faith in the highest sense, and it is up to you if you want to recover. I can only allow it to come to pass." My faith and determined effort to replace defeating self-talk with positive, life-giving truth has literally kept me alive and independent, dealing with my situation every day.

What is your spiritual diet for you like? What do you feed your soul every day? Is it the spiritual diet of an overcomer or the food of a defeatist? Think it over seriously. The next statement I am about to make is so relevant to my recovery. Laughter at the silly or stupid mistakes I would make just trying to relearn how to live again and trying to reestablish that mind-body connection prove to me every day that laughter is a strong immune booster, right along with a positive mental attitude, if that makes sense. Laughter can be great medicine. I remember times a while after having the stroke on my way back to dressing myself, sometimes I would have my shoes on the wrong feet, my shirt would be buttoned wrong, and I would have my pants on backward. Sometimes, I would catch it before I would go out, and I would laugh so hard as I tried to get it straight. I would get it wrong again, but I didn't give up. Eventually, I got it right, but it took years. I am still making mistakes, but what the hell? I'm alive and living independently.

A positive attitude has strengthened me in more ways than I could ever imagine on this journey. Every day, I reseasoned my innermost being, meaning I replaced doubtful, hopeless, negative, and distrustful attitudes embedded in my spirit with real activated trust. Nothing could strengthen me with a sense of well-being like knowing that God kept me here for a reason that maybe I don't even know about yet. He knows my heart and my will to live better than I do. The will affects physiological reality. The will to live has biochemical and physical correlates that have healing power, and the capacity of the human body to regenerate is fantastic, even when the prospects are bleak. God placed in my spirit that I could recover, and I believed it. I worked hard every day. I took personal responsibility for my own therapy, rather than waiting passively for my doctor to make me well even though I had faith in my doctor. He worked as my partner. He was *always* there for me when I called him, but I knew that I had to do the physical work that was required if I wanted to recover. I had to stay focused at all times and keep in mind that faith without *work* is dead.

Keeping a positive attitude and trusting God, I believe I was kept here for a reason. That sounds silly, doesn't it? But it is true. He may use you one day. Do you really believe what you say you do, pertaining to the word? Just think about it. I have come a long way since the stroke. I have been at peace every day. I have never doubted my recovery. I never lost my will. It has been so rewarding. Believe that you can, and you will never declare yourself beaten. Before you start this, belief will keep you from ever trying to beat your illness. This belief will lead to depression. I always keep that winning spirit and believe that sometimes in what we are going through, it is not always the will of God to heal us. Maybe that's why I am handling my condition so well for a godly purpose. I don't proclaim to understand or to know that this can be, but prayer does change things, I believe, to where we can handle them and be at peace wherever we are. That definitely fits me because I am at peace and have always been since the stroke.

I have never been on the verge of giving up. I have discovered a new me, a new hope, and a new way of doing things. It's hard, but amazingly, it feels good to be able and willing to adjust. This is life. Every day, I am feeling better mentally and physically. My speech is getting clearer, and my reading is getting better. It's all because of my attitude. I am experiencing the power of a new and elevated mind-set. It frees me up so I can go on and enjoy new adventures in life. I can increase my physical strength and gain more robust health every day. I am learning that my attitude is the vehicle that keeps elevating me higher and higher in my everyday recovery. I made a promise to myself in the beginning of this journey that no matter how hard the test, I will stay humble and maintain a positive attitude. I cannot travel through this journey within and stand still without what is happening within me affecting what is happening without. The wrong attitude can also affect me like the disease.

If I close my mind when the attitude is positive and conducive to growth, the mind expands and the progress begins. What is the attitude? It is the "advanced man," my true self. The roots are inward, but fruit shows outward. It is our best friend or worst enemy. It is more honest and more consistent than our words. We live in a world of words. Attached to these words are meanings that bring various responses from us. Words such as *happiness, acceptance, peace,* and *success* describe what each of us desires. But there is one word that will either heighten the possibility of our desires being fulfilled or prevent them from becoming a reality within us. What word will describe what determines my happiness? *Attitude*—it's such an important area of our lives, but when we are dealing with a situation, it often gets overlooked. Our attitude is the primary force that will determine whether we succeed or fail. For some, attitude presents a difficulty in every opportunity. For others, it presents an opportunity in every difficulty. Some climb with a positive attitude, while others fail with a negative perspective.

The very fact that the attitude makes some while breaking others, for me, is a challenge of a lifetime—and I do mean a lifetime. I have never been so focused in my life, dealing with something so devastating. My attitude toward my condition from the time I understood what had happened has been excellent. My attitude toward life does not affect society nearly so much as it affects me. The changes cannot come from others. They must come from me, so I press on toward the goal of the prize, which is my recovery. I am individually responsible for my view of my life. Whatever one sows, this one will also reap. Our attitude permits growth through us and our actions toward life. It helps determine in so many ways what happens to us.

God bless. I can do this.

Treasure what you have today, for yesterday
is past. Appreciate the love of family and
friends, for the time they are here.

CPSIA information can be obtained at www.ICGtesting.com
Printed in the USA
LVOW08s1329151215

466711LV00001B/31/P